OAKBOYS

DERRY'S FOOTBALL DREAM COME TRUE

OAKBOYS

DERRY'S FOOTBALL DREAM COME TRUE

EOGHAN CORRY

TORC

First published 1993 by
Torc Books Ltd.
A division of Poolbeg Enterprises Ltd.
Knocksedan House,
123 Baldoyle Industrial Estate, Dublin 13

© Eoghan Corry 1993

The moral right of the author has been asserted.

A catalogue record for this book is available from the British Library.

ISBN 1 898142 10 6

Cover photography David Maher, Sportsfile.
Cover design by PoolbegGroup Services Ltd.
Set by Typeform Repro
Printed by Colour Books, Baldoyle Industrial Estate, Dublin 13.

MARKINGS

We marked the pitch: four jackets for four goalposts,
That was all. The corners and the squares
Were there like longitude and latitude
Under the bumpy thistly ground, to be
Agreed about or disagreed about
When the time came. And then we picked the teams
And crossed the line our called names drew between us.

Youngsters shouting their heads off in a field
As the light died and they kept on playing
Because by then they were playing in their heads
And the actual kicked ball came to them
Like a dream heaviness, and their own hard
Breathing in the dark and skids on grass
Sounded like effort in another world ...
It was quick and constant, a game that never need
Be played out. Some limit had been passed,
There was fleetness, furtherance, untiredness
In time that was extra, unforeseen and free.

Séamus Heaney

An extract from *Markings* from the collection *Seeing Things*, printed in the All-Ireland final programme, 1993, and reproduced by kind permission of Faber and Faber Ltd, London.)

SPERRIN METAL
AND THE DERRY FOOTBALL TEAM

Throughout the past decade and a half, Derry GAA followers continued to celebrate the success of their county minor and under-21 teams at both Ulster and All-Ireland levels.

Now with a nucleus of players from the last victorious Derry side in 1987, combined with such players as Anthony Tohill, Dermot Heaney and Gary Coleman, who have made the successful transition from minor in 1989 to senior level, the Derry team have found the correct combination of youth and experience.

This combination was first recognised and produced fruit last year when Derry defeated old rivals and neighbours Tyrone in the National Football League final in Croke Park. Unfortunately, later in the same year, Derry met eventual All-Ireland kingpins Donegal in the Ulster final and were narrowly beaten by two points.

After Down's All-Ireland win, people within the county decided that a determined effort be made to capture the Sam Maguire. Sound financial back-up would be required, so a finance committee outside the County Board was established and the quest for a sponsor got under way.

Sperrin Metal, the Draperstown-based manufacturer of lockers, shelving and other storage equipment, was the obvious choice. Even at the company's inception in 1963, one of the founders, Father Collins from Draperstown, was also chairman of the County Board and subsequently trained the senior team for several years. Since then, Sperrin has maintained its strong attachment with the board. Over the years, several of the company's employees have represented Derry at different levels, and current left-corner-forward and All-Star Enda Gormley is the nephew of Dr Pat Gormley, Chairman of Sperrin Metal.

Mr William McGinnis, Managing Director of Sperrin and President of the Northern Ireland Chamber of Commerce, outlined the company's continuing interest in the Derry team:

"Sperrin was originally set up as a community project in order to generate employment in the south Derry area and, to a large extent, our corporate culture still reflects our strong links with the local community. From a business point of view, we are obviously aware of the exposure to be gained from a sustained run in the championship, and we are delighted with Derry's win."

Since its foundation in 1963, Sperrin has progressed from a small enterprise to a higly successful export-oriented company with customers in over thirty-five countries throughout the world. The sponsorship of the Derry football team has, however, afforded Sperrin the opportunity to enhance its company profile in its domestic market. This has been reflected in the recent upturn in business generated throughouty the four provinces.

Says leading academic Professor Aidan O'Reilly, Director of Sperrin and ex-Mayo footballer:

"I have witnessed first-hand, during their training sessions at the University of Ulster, the sheer commitment to success that pervades the entire Derry team. This same commitment to success is the underlying factor in Sperrin's development in so many overseas markets."

CONTENTS

PROLOGUE

The journey from Dublin to Maghera on a weekday evening takes a comfortable four hours. For the Derry team returning home on the evening of Monday 20 September 1993 it took twice that. Not that anyone cared: a raucous running party of jubilation ran from town to town, county to county, parish to parish, homeward bound to Derry.

Some of those who travelled with them have seen this kind of party before. Teams win titles, collect cups, have homecoming celebrations; children wave flags, grown men cry. Everybody forgets the troubles of the real world and celebrates for a week: they re-run the video in clubs and shop windows until their eyes are glazed. Meanwhile the rest of the world carries on. It's fun while it lasts, but it is also make-believe.

Perhaps they failed to notice that something more significant was happening this time round. It is not just the bombed-out centre of Magherafelt, the mementoes of death and destruction everywhere. It is that the people from the Sperrins and the Loughshore who have manned Derry teams for generations have had so little to celebrate. The county has had little to celebrate. The Gaelic identity in a divided countryside has had little to celebrate.

"We are not used to winning," Joe Brolly says. "And when we do, there's pandemonium."

For two-thirds of its history, like most of its Ulster neighbours, the Derry football team provided little more than Cavan-fodder in the Ulster championship. Their evolution through perseverance, progress and prosperity is a fascinating tale.

The All-Ireland journey did not begin in Dungiven forty-eight hours beforehand. There are many opinions about where exactly it began. Perhaps at that first team meeting on 6 January. Perhaps in the 1992 League campaign, or Lavey's 1991 triumph; the minor teams and under-21 teams of the 1980s; back in 1958 when Kerry or Cavan were beaten, or the glorious day when Jim McKeever joined the team in 1951; in the mud of Magherafelt when Antrim were beaten in 1946, or half-empty Croke Park, where Clare were beaten in 1947; among the ghosts of the 1902 hurlers of Derry city, or the one-armed pre-GAA hurlers of the Waterside.

Yes, there are record books and newspaper reports to support any of these cases and fill in the details of Derry football, but writing it down can never capture all the story. Reliving football matches can only be done properly when the high field-catches are two feet higher, the free kicks from ten yards further out, and the shoulder of the players two feet broader. The blows struck in passion or pride, the invading crowds and biased referees, the objections and suspensions, sometimes make better telling than chains of All-Irelands.

Derry's achievement belongs to all these people.

1

A TEAM AND A DREAM

A Tyrone footballer once pondered that, should Derry win the All-Ireland, at least they would not need to parade the Sam Maguire Cup through too many towns.

When Derry played Leitrim in a National League match, county PRO Bernie Mullan pointed out that the populations of Limavady and Coleraine probably equalled that of Leitrim. In the dressing-room before the match one of the Derry players added an addendum: "But they're all Catholics in Leitrim, Bernie."

Like an outcrop of measles, Derry's football country was demarcated in red-and-white flags for that merry month of September 1993. As you approached it across the Sperrins, along a road that passed through wide, treeless plains, rocky outcrops and piles of stacked turf, somewhere around the unmarked border between Tyrone and Derry you move into sheepland. This is country for the poor and the papists. The bogs were the preserve of the dispossessed after fate chose Ulster to be the Bosnia of the seventeenth century. Once they were proudly Gaelic by race, now they were proudly Gaelic by sport. The first red-and-white flag greets the stranger a mile beyond the Shepherd's Rest on the Sixtowns road.

Draperstown is the first village you meet on this beautiful route into County Derry. The bunting went up before the All-Ireland semi-final and was to remain up.

Even the name of Draperstown grates on the people of Derry: for this was the parish of Ballinascreen before the Drapers' Company were granted all the property that had been seized from Ó Catháin's kinsmen. Even the Church of Ireland still serves the parish of Ballynascreen, while the GAA's famously tight sports field, Dean McGlinchey Memorial Park at the cross, is definitely Ballinascreen. This is the field in which Gaelic games were preserved when Derry went through its darkest hours.

A few miles beyond Draperstown the road comes to Tobermore, and there is no sign of the bunting. Instead a Union Jack flies at the crossroads. One would be forgiven for thinking that this town is inhabited by disgruntled Tyrone supporters. No, this is "Londonderry"—a different county altogether, a people desperately trying to ignore the All-Ireland final euphoria in their midst.

All through the county the scene is re-enacted, and it quickly becomes clear that there are not just two Derrys but three. GAA Derry is dissipated through the scattered parishes on both sides of the Sperrin Mountains, Dungiven and Glenullin in the north, Maghera, Bellaghy, Desertmartin, Ballymaguigan, Ballinderry and Gulladuff in the south, which provided the GAA teams of the past forty years in Derry. Soccer Derry lies to the north-west. Londonderry, its heart and mind dedicated to Belfast and Whitehall, straddles both territories. Bunting betrays the GAA Derry: the red-and-white flags fly only in areas where they are safe from the wrath of loyalists. In Maghera the bunting comes to a halt half way down the main street.

One of the pubs on the wrong side of town belongs to a Derry footballer.

Glenullin, where the team trains, a townland that won the club championship in 1985, does not appear on any map. Nor does the home of All-Ireland club title winners in 1991, Lavey. The St Mary's parish bulletin has "Ireland's premier parish" on its masthead from that time. Ballymaguigan, whence came Jim McKeever and current team manager Éamonn Coleman, is another village of 1,000 people. It is in the parish of Magherafelt, which supports four of the traditionally strongest clubs in Derry football. "Derry football comes from a small number of parishes," Anthony Tohill says. "It gives you a great sense of belonging when you feel you can do something for your local people."

To find the Oakboys in preparation, first you had to find Glenullin. Glenwhere? The directions from Swatragh were accurate enough. Turn left, then right, and follow the road until you know you are really lost. Then look to your left and you can't miss the GAA field.

This is a Unionist council area, so no grants were available for Glenullin's breathtaking mountain pitch. Drained and landscaped, it comes with a massive hall, stand, dressing-rooms, and function rooms, and £24,000 worth of floodlights. They play hurling under floodlights here, and train Derry teams in two codes and six grades throughout the year. It is not unique: Bellaghy's complex is equally daunting, and the forty-two active clubs are all well provided with facilities. "Look at Glenullin," Joe Brolly says. "Nobody lives here, nothing worth talking about, and you would never go through it or anything. Good focus and good people. And they built this all by themselves."

Joe's father, Francie Brolly, told Éamonn McCann in the *Sunday Tribune* in August 1993: "The nationalist people here tend to see themselves as surrounded, hemmed in and not able to express themselves freely in public affairs. In that situation the GAA came to play a tremendously important role."

The plush new centres have sometimes attracted the wrong sort of attention. Glenullin's club premises were constructed entirely with voluntary labour, and as soon as they were finished they were damaged in a fire started by members of the Ulster Defence Association, who came up to vent their spleen. A complex in Swatragh suffered the same fate. But in many ways Derry GAA enjoys an easy ride—none of the victimisation of Tyrone players, detained for questioning on training nights in the run-up to the 1986 All-Ireland, or the detention of the entire Antrim hurling team on their way to a training session before the 1989 All-Ireland. The problems of seeking sponsorship have not been as marked as in their Six Counties neighbours, where corporate business is hesitant to become associated with an organisation that draws such loyalist wrath on itself. Sperrin Metal have purchased some valuable jersey space; a Kilrea electrical dealer has underwritten some major development projects; and the ambitious new training complex in Dungiven, a four-pitch centre that will be the envy of north and south alike, has found many willing supporters.

The GAA in Northern Ireland has survived all this and

has avoided being skewered on the axis between constitutional and violent nationalism. There are reminders
everywhere of the intrusion of tragedy, heartbreak, and
violence. One of Derry's All-Ireland captains of the past,
Kevin Lynch of an under-16 hurling team that won a
championship for developing hurling counties, later died
on hunger-strike, and the Dungiven hurling club was
renamed in his honour. A brother of the great 1970s
midfielder Tom McGuinness, one of the last Derry city
players, was elected to the 1982 Northern Assembly and is
a leading figure in Sinn Féin. In a move motivated by
compassion rather than any ideological statement, three
youngsters killed by their own bomb in a premature
explosion—Sheridan, Bateson, and Lee—had the memorial
cup for the Derry intermediate championship named after
them in 1971.

In these sad circumstances, Derry deserved their
celebration. Albeit in its sectarian straitjacket, the football
fever is palpable. One can see the red-and-white bunting
offering a chance of public celebration that would never be
accorded other nationalist symbols. Children wearing
Derry jerseys walk openly in the streets. Conversation in
the bars on the right side of town was about Derry football,
the full-back question, tickets, and the value of the secret
stock of reserves, men like Dermot McNicholl and Declan
Bateson.

A cousin of goalkeeper Damien McCusker's recorded a
team song that will not win any awards, even by the
usually musically challenged standards of these
compositions, but some radio stations chose to fade the

last verse about the cup being interrogated by a British soldier.

There are signs that the unionists too are proud of their team. By beating the best the Free State has to offer, Down's and Derry's victories confirm a peculiar unionist theory: asserting Ulster's superiority over the detested Free State. Many have shown an interest in getting tickets, but there were no unionist politicians at the 1993 All-Ireland final. Willie Ross, the East Derry MP, is a highly respected and supportive politician. His brother carried out the GAA's printing work for many years. The unionist town of Garvagh hosted many of the Glenullin visitors on Tuesday. Before the troubles there were Protestant players; even an RUC man lines out incognito with a north Derry club. Strangely enough, as long as he did not play soccer nobody objected.

Such ecumenism would be unthinkable now. A television crew from BBC arrived at a training session before the final, attempting to ask the players about the RUC ban. They met with no respondents at the Tuesday training session. Although cross-community relations are not comparable to the sectarian tit-for-tat of Belfast, and there has been no recent equivalent of the attacks on north Down GAA clubs, Glenullin is not far away from the loyalist gunmen who regard footballers of the wrong code as legitimate targets.

In terms of resources, it should have been no contest at all. Derry have 41 clubs, Cork 262. Derry have 66 adult and

106 youth football teams; Cork's totals of 267 adult and 605 youth football teams are the highest in Ireland, running 50 per cent ahead of the comparable statistics for Dublin.

But the demographics don't take commitment into account. "Compared with Cork, we certainly did not have the selection that Cork would have," team captain Henry Downey says. "But what we do have is good quality. Quality is more important than quantity." When players talk about the standards of having only three or four strong clubs competing in the local championships, they gloss over the fact that two Derry clubs have won All-Ireland club championships—Lavey two years ago and Bellaghy back in 1972; a third, Ballerin, also reached an All-Ireland final in 1976, and Ballinderry won the Ulster championship in 1981. Three minor All-Irelands and three colleges titles, two under-21 finals and two club and two National League titles and an astounding minor hurling performance against Kilkenny, losing a semi-final by just three points two years ago, are performances that defy the demographics. Derry's ability to field teams that have done the business has been an astounding facet of football life in the county. In this respect they almost exactly resemble Down, who won an All-Ireland in 1991.

In the circumstances there are not enough players to go around for other codes as well, and Gerry McElhinney and Martin O'Neill, both of whom played for Northern Ireland soccer teams in the 1980s, proved grievous losses. Two more lost to the game in the 1980s, Eddie McElhinney, younger brother of Gerry, and especially

Declan McNicholl, cousin of Dermot, would be sorely missed in these circumstances.

Not only the game has changed. The resources of a community were mobilised with one end in mind. In doing so, they changed the course of GAA history for themselves, the one-third of a county they represent, and maybe a few of the other two-thirds as well.

There were those who did not share the euphoria. The supporters' club shop in Maghera was broken into and wrecked on the night of the final. Supporters returning home were set upon by a group of about 150 loyalists in Cookstown.

Almost all the Derry players admit that they got more emotional after the Dublin match. The final was too tense, and did not require a comeback from behind. Many ticket-holders were punching the air, not on Hill 16 but in the public houses nearby. The gates were closed half an hour before the senior match, because the crush was too great, and many who travelled to Dublin saw it on telly instead.

The journey home posed dangers of its own. Cookstown is a divided town. You can tell the Catholic end by the army checkpoints. By eleven o'clock on Sunday night a group of unionists, fortified with passion and porter, had begun to gather with clubs and Union Jacks at the top of the town, the Oldtown end, to menace traffic returning from the match.

Over the next hour, Derry supporters were forced to run the gauntlet. Near the top of the town a car carrying red-and-white flags would pull out and drive in front of the traffic. After they had gone through the traffic lights they would brake suddenly, forcing the Derry cars to stop, and then the gang would emerge from the Munarush area, smashing windows and kicking side panels. The RUC decided not to intervene, perhaps for their own safety; but one policeman, when asked why they were doing nothing, said, "We didn't ask you to come through here." Other officers re-routed traffic round the town, through the less confrontational unionist territory of Beechway.

For the team, Cookstown was one of eleven stops on the longest journey home in All-Ireland history. This time Saracens were parked across the road to block the trouble-makers, and the victory parade was diverted around the estate. Cookstown, tucked four miles inside the Tyrone border, normally has no love for Derry until the Ulster championship comes to an end. When the Derry team came through, they celebrated as they might have done in 1986.

Donegal had a great welcome after they won the Sam Maguire in 1992, but they got home before it started. Somehow, before the team bus had even left County Meath one could get the feeling that this was not going to be the case with Derry. The first flags were out in Balbriggan, twenty miles north of Dublin. One old man walked half a mile with his walking-stick to stand by his gateposts and see the bus fly by. A stop in Dundalk, a stop on the border that the GAA's *Treoraí Oifigiúil* does not recognise, a welcome in Newry worthy of their 1991 predecessors, a stop in Plunkett Donaghy's home town, Moy in County Tyrone and, exhausted, in Magherafelt. The fireworks were set off to signify their arrival in Maghera, the final stop, at 3:05 a.m. on Tuesday morning. The first Bank of Ireland posters, "Derry, All-Ireland champions", had been on sale since teatime. One of those who looked on in wonder was Karl Diamond's grandfather, John Joe Diamond. "Thank God for sparing me to live to see the day," he said. Then he added: "And I'm sure he'll spare me to see a few more as well."

Nobody estimates street crowds properly. The crowd in Maghera ranged between fifteen and thirty thousand, depending on which newspaper you read. Most people who were there remember the long and joyous wait as well as the arrival. A blind eye was turned on the licensing laws by a highly co-operative RUC, who had announced that they would field a GAA team in a week if the ban on participation was lifted.

Bringing the cup home, even in winning counties, is always hyped up as the biggest party yet. Every year is said to be better than the last. But first-time winners go completely over the top by tradition. Joe Brolly reckoned one of Derry's problems was that there is no tradition of winning, "and when we do, it's pandemonium." Galway in 1980 was one to recall. Donegal's homecoming in 1992 was reckoned to be the best by the very people who were now awarding the honour to Derry. And nobody ever before made as many stops on the way.

In truth there is little difference. Celebration is celebration. People get emotional or drunk, or both. Offaly hurlers in 1981 got that special welcome when they came back to their heartland: the hurling parishes in the west. Derry too have their hinterland, the parishes of the south, and that is where they arrived on Monday night. This is the place to which Aodh Ó Néill retreated after the Battle of Kinsale, to be among his own. They have rarely been on the winning side since. And that was what made Tuesday morning 21 September 1993 so special in the Sperrins.

On Tuesday it was Dungiven's turn, the land of Brollys and McGilligans and McKeevers. The RUC press office telephoned the BBC to find out who exactly this Maguire chap was and why he was called Samuel. (A Cork Protestant who headed IRA intelligence in Britain during the War of Independence, a cohort of Michael Collins. Another of those bloody quirks of Irish history, they comment.)

Bellaghy's ground can only hold nine thousand people. The extent of the problem this caused was apparent early on Wednesday afternoon, when people began gathering for Derry v. Rest of Ireland. This is an annual event in aid of the Third World charity GOAL, started by Dublin sports writer John O'Shea. An estimated twelve thousand showed, a little higher than the record attendance for this series, recorded in heavy rain in Ballybofey in 1992. John O'Shea reckons the attendance was four times what it would be in any of the other three provinces. It is not a real match, played in an idealised, rarefied atmosphere in which the home team has already won and all that's left to do is cheer them all the way to the final whistle and a humorous commentary: "It's a big success for the pan-nationalist front." The Rest of Ireland always wins, and the biggest cheer of the evening came when their manager, Brian McEniff, came on and scored a point.

This was the children's night. At half time they come on with their flags to dance around after the Faughanvale GAC accordion band. The pitch is engulfed by pint-sized flag-carriers who sweep on to get autographs and pose with toothless grins for the camera with famous footballers. Veteran Meath player Colm O'Rourke is a special favourite; he gives away tee-shirts and takes time with them all. Football life carries on. Éamonn Coleman's son Vivian turns up with a swollen thumb from a match earlier the same evening. They have come from all over the county, and despite a few officious gentlemen ordering children off the field, everybody goes home happy, even John O'Shea.

Players sometimes don't manage the celebrations well. Offaly 1982 hero Séamus Darby says the All-Ireland celebrations lasted a year for him and cost him a fortune. It's only a fortnight to the first round of the National League, you see. But Derry are treating this whole celebration like an extended period of extra time, testing their stamina with being back-slapped and cheered, but so far they haven't had a single relaxing drink. Lots of dinners, lots of speeches, and a thousand autographs to sign. Being idolised carries responsibility as well, Colm O'Rourke told the players. "The young people here are the future of the GAA in Derry."

2

THE PLAYERS AND THEIR COUNTY

Like any assault on a famous summit, there are many base camps for this Derry All-Ireland expedition. Some trace the journey back to base camp Clones, when Derry players, having done all the hard work by beating All-Ireland champions Down, cruelly lost to Donegal in the 1992 provincial final. Defeat concentrates the mind, and the eyes narrow as each of the players discusses the pain, the physically sick feeling of that evening and the following weeks.

There was also base camp Toomebridge, a meeting on 6 January of this year that aired all the criticisms and differences among the panel and selectors. Hard things were said that day; everybody had an opinion on what was wrong with Derry's approach, and stock was taken. "You know, even before the panel was selected we had a team meeting," Brian McGilligan pondered. "We said we are as good as Down and Donegal, who have both won the Sam Maguire, so let's give it everything." "We decided to give 100 per cent," Gary Coleman says. "Girls, night-clubs, drink—everything goes out the window for one crack at this All-Ireland; that's all sometimes you get."

Then there was base camp Croke Park, when everything was going wrong in the All-Ireland semi-final and Dublin were leading by ten points to four. Selector Mickey Moran did a Cú Chulainn-like war spasm in the dressing-room that day. The players had thirty-five minutes to redeem themselves.

To win an All-Ireland you need good management. As managers go, Éamonn Coleman's passion, wit and love for his county were renowned long before Derry hit the big time. "He wants to be manager, full-back, midfield, corner-forward, and referee, all at the same time," Meath footballer Colm O'Rourke once said. In February 1991 he returned from the building sites of London to manage the team.

Born in the small town of Ballymaguigan, an only son, with three sisters and a father who had little or no interest in the game, Éamonn was only a gasún in 1958 when Derry went to the All-Ireland. He didn't get to the match, but he remembers flying a flag on a pole at home. In the summer of 1962, at fourteen years of age, Éamonn Coleman played his first game of senior championship football, and he swears he wasn't one bit afraid.

His opponents were Ballymaguigan's great rivals from the same parish, Castledawson. In the county semi-final Jim McKeever, one of the outstanding sons raised on Derry's Gaelic football fields, didn't care to risk young Coleman. Bellaghy and Ballymaguigan were old rivals from inter-district days. Coleman was still in national school.

In the county final, Éamonn Coleman's schoolmaster, Felix Mackle, was playing corner-forward for Castledawson. Having come on at half time, Éamonn scored a point, and the game ended in a draw; added a goal and a point in the replay, and Ballymaguigan won its only Derry senior football championship.

At that stage Coleman was quick on his feet, and he was hard to hit. If somebody did hit him they probably would have buried him all right, but he had Jim McKeever and the boys playing alongside. Jim looked after him.

He had a brief reminder the following summer, when Bellaghy right-corner-back Kevin Mulholland hit him with everything he had in a championship game, fair and square, not dirty. But he thought he was going to die. He lay there and cried like a wee boy.

Éamonn's mother had died the year before he played his first game for Ballymaguigan. His father earned his money through labouring, farm work, roads, buildings, but the family also had a few cattle. One day Éamonn was building a garage for someone and went straight after work to the football field. At home a cow was lost in calf. His father cursed football from a height.

Derry won an All-Ireland minor championship in 1965 and an under-21 championship in 1968 with Éamonn on the team. When they won their second minor title in 1983 Éamonn Coleman was manager of the team. Ten years later he was manager of the Derry team that won the Sam Maguire Cup for the first time. In the dressing-room in Newry before they played Down in the first round of the championship he told the team he had given them everything he had got. "I've given them everything I have in the last three years almost, money-wise, everything. I told them it was now up to them to win the All-Ireland. I could do no more for them."

To win an All-Ireland you need strength in depth. Derry's

1993 panel had something that no previous county team could claim: a strong panel. True, the names were familiar. True, they came from the familiar clubs of four parishes. But they were dispensable, with capable replacements in case of injury.

"The players are out there who want to make this team," team captain Henry Downey says. "And it is very difficult to make a Derry panel now. Players that aren't on the panel are really trying very hard to make it."

"Seeing Down win an All-Ireland and seeing Donegal win an All-Ireland has put that wee bit more bite into the team, a wee bit more appetite," says Danny Quinn. "The competition for places is fierce. The training is intense and there has been 90 per cent effort all the time. Competition for places is the big thing. In 1987 the disappointing thing was Dermot McNicholl got injured. I think that took a wee bit out of the team. I think now we can afford some of our better players to get injured and it is not going to take anything out of it, because we have that strong a panel. It is a relief to make the nine substitutes now at the minute for a final, because there is that big a competition for places. It is a bigger relief to get on."

The Oakboys evident in parts of the city this week might not think so, but John McGurk agrees. "After 1987 they hadn't the confidence to go on and be a great team. They were a good team at that stage, but they were lacking leadership or something. The present-day team would have had a lot more leaders than Derry would have had then. Nearly all players you speak to out there are leaders on the pitch today, whereas in 1987 none of the players were really encouraged to grab the game by the scruff of the neck. Plus the panel today is better than any panel Derry ever had. You are talking about twenty-five players that are always going to be in there with a chance of the fifteen places. That encourages great competition."

Perhaps it is the small population, but the story of Derry football is full of names that skip a generation and recur, and great family names. Four Gribbens played together for the 1950s teams, seven McGurks helped Lavey to an All-Ireland club title in 1991. Harry Cassidy, father of Damien, was a 1958 hero and the manager of a famous 1973 team that drew with Kerry in a riotous League semi-final and failed to show up for the replay because the same referee was reappointed.

Like their 1958 predecessors, these are professionals: three teachers, an accountant, a barrister, and a civil engineer; seven players who played third-level football for the Sigerson Cup, and earlier with St Patrick's College in Maghera. "Colleges football teaches you about dedication, the amount of dedication you need to win," Danny Quinn says. "Sigerson football teaches you about training. It's amazing the amount of training it takes to win a Sigerson, up to four nights a week."

Goalkeeper Damien McCusker, a 26-year-old from Glen, stands 6 feet 1 inch and weighs 14 stone. He works as a civil servant, and played outfield at all levels of football, playing midfield for his club and winning senior, under-21 Railway Cup and National League medals in goal with

Derry. John J. McKenna from the Maghera club introduced him to football at under-10 and under-12 level. Damien started in goal, kicking about with his friends and his brothers and playing in goal for primary school teams. In different age groups he was in goal one year and outfield the next. He played in goal for St Patrick's College teams that won Ulster championships in 1982, 1983, and 1984. It continued like that until he joined the county senior team off the minor team in the 1984/85 National League season.

It was in the salubrious surroundings of Tubbercurry, against Sligo in Division 3 of the League, that he made his debut. It was before Christmas and it was very cold. "I remember the goalmouth—half of it was a pool of water." He thinks a little, then adds: "That said, it was probably better than Clones for the 1993 Ulster senior final." Goalkeepers remember these things.

Becoming a county goalkeeper at seventeen is unusual. "Minor players probably don't think there is a lot of difference between what they play and senior football, but you are dealing with men. It is quicker and a much more physical game. Beating Down last year was my favourite memory, because they had beaten us the year before." He did not think he had a serious save to make since the Down match, and he made two saves and he hasn't had a serious shot against him since then.

Kieran McKeever from Dungiven was twenty-four at the time of the final, just 5 feet 7 in height and 11 stone weight. He worked as a joiner and had already been nominated twice for an All-Star award, earning a reputation as one of the game's tightest markers. He captained the 1986 Derry minor team beaten by Down in the Ulster final. Out-thinking a forward who thinks he's clever is his speciality, and Derry people thrill to see the corner-back coming out of his defence with the ball. He was sent off against Donegal in the 1993 league quarter-final defeat, never having been sent off in his life before. What happened was unfortunate. His head was down and he was defending himself. He could have hit the other player on the backside for all he knew.

Fergal McCusker from the Maghera club, Glen, stands 5 feet 11, weighs 12 stone 3. A 23-year-old bank official, he is the younger brother of goalkeeper Damien. He had made his senior debut at the age of seventeen, and earned a reputation for his ability to play either in defence or attack. He was discovered by team manager Tom Scullion in 1988 when he was a surprise choice in a National League play-off against Armagh, scoring a goal that helped stave off relegation. Fergal is regarded as one of the best minors to play for the county.

Tony Scullion from Ballinascreen is thirty-one, stands 5 feet 11 and weighs 12 stone 7. A veteran of ten years on the Derry side, he switched to full-back in that semi-final against Dublin and curbed Vinny Murphy, who was causing a lot of damage. By the time of the All-Ireland he already had two All-Star awards, for 1987 and 1992, had five Railway Cup medals, National League and Ulster under-21 awards, man of the match awards in the Ulster finals of 1987 and 1992, and had played twice against

Australia. He first came to notice when he played under-21 in his last year of eligibility in 1983.

John McGurk from Lavey was twenty-seven at the time of the All-Ireland, stands a mere 5 feet 7 (Derry's official information claimed 5 feet 6), and weighs 11 stone. One of two survivors from the All-Ireland 1983 minor winning team, he had won the Ulster championship in 1987 and the National League in 1992. "I used to play forward for my club, but I played all my football for Derry at right-half-back. You are often in various attacks as a half-back, so if you get a chance to shoot you are used to shooting, and our half-backs usually do have a go at the goal."

He is fifteen years younger than his All-Star brother. "The first match I remember Anthony playing was the 1973 National League semi-final against Kerry. I was sitting in the Hogan Stand. It was desperate. I remember my sister writing an essay about it. That's how bad it was: even my sister was writing about football. The next game after that was about 1975; I can remember the Ulster final when they beat Down, and they won it again in 1976. It was terrible, because we had grown up to believe that Derry could win anything really, and they lost to very good sides at that stage. That was a very good Derry team, only it happened to arrive when Dublin and Kerry were at their best. The Derry team of that era would probably have won a few All-Irelands in the present day. They were a big, strong side."

John made his club debut at fifteen, and his county debut at nineteen, in 1985. Himself and Enda Gormley made their debut together in the National League match against Antrim at Corrigan Park, John at left-half-forward, Enda at left-corner-forward.

Henry Downey, also from Lavey, captained the 1993 All-Ireland team at the age of twenty-six. A teacher, he is 5 feet 9 and 12 stone. He was an All-Star nominee in 1992. Unusually for a team that had grown up together in public, he had not shared in the heroics at minor and under-21 levels, and first played for Derry seniors in 1988. A dual player, he once broke his leg playing football.

A lot of people felt in 1992 that he was too adventurous for centre-half. He was running all over the place, but in 1993 he outplayed Ray McCarron, Greg Blaney and Martin McHugh in the Ulster championship. And as captain, he showed great leadership qualities on the field. In the Ulster final Brian McCormick was suffering, because the first three balls went by McCormick and he just kicked them. Henry came in and had a word in his ear, and the next ball that Brian McCormick got was run. The victory speech of 19 September 1993 was far from his mind when he watched the 1992 All-Ireland on television. "The Derry club championship is very competitive, and there is no guarantee that if you win it one year you are going to the next year. With four or five strong clubs scoring off each other, the standard improved over a couple of years, first of all because of Lavey and then because of Derry winning the National League. Every game we played through that 1993 championship, we got better as we went along. It put this fearsome confidence in this team."

Gary Coleman from Magherafelt was just twenty-one at the time of the All-Ireland, working as a postman, standing 5 feet 9 and weighing 11 stone 6. He had oceans of under-age experience, having captained Derry minors to two Ulster championships and an All-Ireland championship. His pedigree was impeccable, the son of team manager Éamonn Coleman, nephew of one of Éamonn's 1965 All-Ireland minor and 1968 under-21 winning team-mates on his mother's side. "I wanted to emulate everything they had done from an early age, and I have been lucky at minor, under-21, and senior." The luck was augmented with running skills and patience. "Gary must be an awful player to have to play against," his father, Éamonn, says. "No matter how many times Gary gets hit he never lifts his hand."

Anthony Tohill from Swatragh is big. At sixteen he was over 6 feet tall. Significantly, he is also the player whom former star Jim McKeever likes most on the 1993 Derry team. "He does not need his height. If he was a smaller player he would still be as good." A towering 6 feet 4½ inches, he weighs 14 stone 10 lbs. The skill was slower in coming than the height. He played one year for Derry minors and was substituted against Cavan. A 22-year-old student, he was one of three Derry men to win an All-Star award in 1992. Anthony's performance for Queen's in a Sigerson semi-final a few years ago is still talked about. His appetite whetted by the epic colleges encounter with St Colman's of Newry, which St Patrick's of Maghera won by 4-10 to 4-9 in 1989, at eighteen Anthony went to Australia and played Australian rules as an apprentice with Melbourne for a while. "At the time it was too good an opportunity to say no. Things didn't work out, but it was still great to go out there and see another country, and to play semi-professional football was great. If they had, I probably wouldn't have had to worry about money for the rest of my life." He learnt to hand-pass with both hands, and came home with a huge muscular frame that nobody can ignore. On the night he returned he went straight to the Derry training camp. He won Ulster and All-Ireland minor medals before he went, and returned to win National League and Railway Cup medals. In 1992 he scored 2-8 out of 2-10 for Swatragh when they beat Bellaghy for the first time in club competition, and even bested Brian McGilligan when the partners met in the club championship. After the 1993 Ulster final Brian McEniff declared he was the best footballer in Ireland.

His father played for Swatragh but never got a chance to play for the county. But he introduced his son to Gaelic at an early age. He played with Swatragh at primary level.

Brian McGilligan from Dungiven is just an inch smaller, 6 feet $3\frac{1}{2}$, and weighs in at 14 stone 10. At twenty-nine Brian was the third-oldest on the 1993 All-Ireland side, behind Tony Scullion and Damien Barton. He was working as a site foreman in the Creggan at the time of the All-Ireland and had attracted a considerable supporters' club of local youngsters. Unusually for Derry's 1993 All-Ireland team, he never played inter-county minor, and first came to notice in the 1982 county final when he punched a spectacular winning goal for Dungiven in the last minute of the county final against Magherafelt.

Brian was virtually unknown outside Derry when Kevin Heffernan telephoned him in America to pick him for the Australian tour in 1986, and he spent the summer training with the Tyrone All-Ireland team under Art McRory to get into shape for the series. That tour played an important part in his development, taught him a lot about training, about coaching, about tactics. He first played for Derry in 1982, but it was four years before he established himself, and then promptly won an All-Star award.

Rated an even better hurler, in 1983 he was told by Brian Cody that he would be good enough to make the Kilkenny team. Brian has won seven hurling and four football county championships, but comes out second-best in the medals table in his own household. His wife, Bríd O'Doherty, is the holder of fourteen senior camogie championship medals with Swatragh. She was captain of the camogie team and he the captain of the hurling team in the year they married.

He still reckons hurling is a much more manly game. "You don't get nearly as much feigning of injury in hurling. But I just could not combine the two, because of the commitment involved."

By his own admission, Brian never liked training. "It wasn't that I didn't want to train, but after a hard day's work it wasn't easy to go straight out and get into a hard training session. I used to think I was fit then, and I was a stone heavier than now. It seems to get harder and harder each year, the amount of work and effort you have to put into it increase every time the championship comes round.

When we are out sprinting these young boys are trying to make a name for themselves, so you can't sit back. It just got bigger and bigger as we got closer and closer to winning something big, and when we did it in the National League it was incredible. I thought we had trained hard for that, but you should see what we had to do in 1993. When you think of the amount of time you put in, the long hours since February, sometimes you wonder is it worth it, and now you see that it is.

"We always had doubts in our minds about what we could do, but when we saw Down and Donegal win the All-Ireland we knew it was not pie in the sky any more. We were geared for the National League in 1992. We won that and lost to Donegal in the championship. The League meant nothing then."

Dermot Heaney from Castledawson was just twenty-two, stands 6 feet tall, weighs 13 stone, and was a store manager. By fifteen, Dermot was regarded as a football prodigy, and played three years at minor level. He first played at midfield and was moved then to full-forward for a successful spell there. He went into the All-Ireland final with the enviable record of never having lost at Croke Park. He played on the minor team that won the 1989 All-Ireland semi-final and final, the senior team that won the 1992 League semi-final and final, and on winning teams against Dublin in October 1992 and August 1993. In 1992 he had played midfield for Derry the previous year but then moved back to the attack. He pulled a hamstring before the Ulster final. "It didn't bother me during the game but I knew in my heart I wasn't right, and the conditions were probably what really ruined my day, not doing either the team or myself any justice, and I asked to be taken off."

Damien Barton from Newbridge was 6 feet tall, weighed 13 stone, and had spent some thirteen seasons with Derry. His debut was in the 1981 Ulster championship semi-final alongside such as Mark McFeeley, Mickey Moran and Anthony McGurk when he came on as a substitute for Jim McGroarty. Derry were beaten 0-12 to 0-9 in that match. A 31-year-old schoolteacher in St Patrick's in Dungannon, he was the only survivor from the spate of Vocational Schools successes that Derry had enjoyed in the early 1980s. He won Ulster minor, under-21 and eventually an Ulster senior medal in 1987. Damien captained Derry in Croke Park as a minor and under-21.

Damien Cassidy from Bellaghy stood 5 feet 9, weighed 12 stone, and worked as a social worker in County Armagh. He was twenty-seven at the time of the All-Ireland. "Winning an All-Ireland takes maturity. I didn't think we were good enough to beat Down when we played in the Ulster final in 1991. On the other hand, when we lost to Donegal in 1992 I think we were possibly good enough to win. We got a little more experience, and watching both Down and Donegal win the All-Ireland has helped remove any mental block we might have had about being able to win it. And now we have won it, we should be around for a while. Myself and McNicholl are only twenty-seven, the oldest player is thirty-one, and it is a young squad."

Joe Brolly from Dungiven stands 5 feet 10, weighs 12 stone, and at twenty-four had just started practising on the Northern Circuit as a barrister. His parents, Francie and Ann Brolly, were folk singers and collectors of music. It was very much a Gaelic household. His grandfather was one of the prime movers in the Dungiven club. His father played in a couple of championship matches for Derry, scoring two goals against Fermanagh. Gaelic football was part of life. Joe played Sigerson Cup football with both Queen's and Trinity, where he played on the 1990 Trinity College team that enjoyed a great championship run.

"They play a great style of football in Dublin club football. It would be a much better standard of club football in Dublin than it would be in Derry. They are much more evenly based. There are only a few teams in Derry. I am amazed that players whose only experience is club football in Derry can play at such high levels: McGilligan, McKeever, Scullion; I find it unbelievable. Henry Downey and those boys would have university football behind them, which gives you a whole new range of skills."

As Derry hurling crusader Liam Hinphy is married to his aunt, it was only natural that he played hurling, featuring on Dungiven Féile na nGael teams. Peter Stevenson taught in the local school, so it was all football and hurling, particularly hurling. He was an absolute hurling fanatic. "The hurling fizzled out, because there is plenty of glamour attached to the football but none to hurling. It attracts the young people."

Séamus Downey from Lavey, a former county hurling captain, got a surprise call-up for the All-Ireland semi-final against Dublin. He stands 6 feet tall and weighs 13 stone 5. The full-forward throughout 1992, he came down with cruciate ligament and knee injuries and then tore a hamstring holidaying with Lavey at Christmas.

As a result he was not considered among the first twenty-one for three 1983 championship outings in Ulster. He last appeared for Derry as a substitute in the National League against Dublin when they beat them in October 1992.

Enda Gormley, from the Maghera club, Glen, stands 5 feet 10, weighs 13 stone 4, and was twenty-six at the time of the All-Ireland success. He had won two Sigerson Cup medals with Queen's, and was top scorer in the 1992 Ulster championship. He is no relation of 1958 goalkeeper Patsy, but to Brian Mullan, right-corner-forward in 1958. He never saw Brian play, but remembers watching another uncle, Colm P. Mullan, playing in the early 1970s. He was later tragically paralysed in a car crash.

"When I started taking football seriously my father and I fell out big time. It did not matter if there were ten thousand people at a match, I heard him. We came to an agreement: don't discuss me, discuss everybody else. A bit critical, so he was. My uncles would not be a bit shy about telling me, which is a good thing; my friends are the exact same. The fellows I run about with would not be afraid to tell me how I played."

He went to Australia when Anthony Tohill and Dermot McNicholl were both out there, training with Australian football teams to get over his first bad injury, having torn cruciate ligaments in both knees. Having got away with it on his left knee for four years now he hopes to be equally lucky with his right. The leg went just after the 1992 Ulster final when he was playing in the club championship, and he went to the English FA treatment centre in Lilleshall in February 1993 for treatment.

Football helped get him his job as a representative for a finance company, Northern Bank Leasing, in the south Derry area. "I suppose being known well in the local area was a factor. Football certainly does no harm. It stands you out from the rest of the crowd, there are so many people going for jobs nowadays. Every employer is looking for that wee bit extra. It shows in that way. It gets you through doors; what you do when you're through them is up to yourself."

The club has not been doing well. "Maghera has always had good representation on Derry teams, but it just never pulled it off at senior championship level. The club has died a bit in recent years."

With the first generation of St Patrick's College stars he won the 1984 Ulster championship, after losing seven of their Ulster Colleges team through the difference in age regulations at the time. Five of the 1993 All-Ireland panel went on to get beaten in the All-Ireland final by St Jarlath's of Tuam: Dermot McNicholl, Colm McGurk, Colm Rafferty, Cathal McNicholl, and Danny Quinn.

Enda is free-taker with the team. "You always try to get a few early kicks in and a good strike of the ball. When you miss an easy one it is essential to concentrate. Just get the head back down before the next ball and concentrate. But I just feel they are two totally different aspects of my game. One won't affect the other. There were days when I have got rave reviews for scoring seven, eight, nine points and coming in thinking I had a terrible game."

Don Kelly of Ballinascreen made his name at Croke Park in September 1983 with a spectacular penalty save from Teddy McCarthy in the All-Ireland minor final. Aged twenty-seven, he was 5 feet 10 in height and 11 stone, playing as understudy to Damien McCusker in the Derry goals.

Danny Quinn from Bellaghy had enjoyed seven great years as Derry full-back when he was disappointingly dropped for the All-Ireland final after a protracted debate about the full-back position. Aged twenty-six, he worked as a teacher. He had stayed as Derry's full-back for seven good years after a remarkable medal-winning progression through the ranks. His father had not played inter-county football but he was a fanatical follower of Bellaghy club, for which Danny and his brother John played up through the ranks. John also played inter-county minor and under-21. Danny went to St Patrick's College in Maghera, winning three McRory titles but heartbreakingly losing a Hogan Cup final to St Jarlath's, Tuam.

For a time in the mid-1980s, Danny thought the medals would never stop coming: a minor All-Ireland winner in 1983, an Ulster minor medal in 1984, two Ulster under-21s in 1985 and 1986, and an Ulster senior championship in 1987. "We have had good players the whole way through.

It's just getting it gelled right together. We put in a lot more effort." In St Mary's College in Belfast to train as a teacher, alongside Séamus Downey, he starred on a college team that was coached by 1950s hero Jim McKeever and Peter Finn. Gaelic football's premier colleges trophy, the Sigerson Cup, had just been opened to non-university teams, and Danny and friends were determined to win it. "We played well together, and played well as a team. We beat UUJ, Galway, in the quarter-final, Queen's in the semi-final, and played Maurice FitzGerald's Cork team in the final, on one of those days everything went right. A lot of the boys were playing county football, like Jarlath Burns from Armagh, Fergal McCann from Fermanagh, John Reihill from Fermanagh, Malachy O'Rourke from Fermanagh, John Rafferty from Armagh, so we had a fair sprinkling of county men through it. We were the first St Mary's team to win the Sigerson Cup and probably the last, just because of the numbers. There are not many boys in the college. At the time there were twenty-four or twenty-five footballers on our panel and we fared well with injury. There were only one or two injuries during the Sigerson run."

The best game he ever had was in the National League semi-final against Meath in 1991, one of those days that full-backs dream about. "Full-back is a funny position. It depends on how you are doing out the field. If your midfield is doing well, if your half-forwards are playing well, what percentage of what comes in is quality ball can determine your performance. If pressure is put on the man kicking the ball, it gives you a fifty-fifty chance. But if the midfield or the half-backs are getting a chance to look up and place their ball there is very little a defender can do. I think that is why I suffered a bit in the first fifteen minutes of the All-Ireland semi-final against Dublin. They had a chance to look up and play the ball again. As the game went on, Tohill and McGilligan dominated midfield in the second half, and the ball going in to the Dublin forwards was not as good as the ball going in in those opening minutes: it wasn't quality ball. That's what made the difference. It makes it easier for the defender."

Karl Diamond from Bellaghy stands 5 feet 9, weighs 12 stone, and at twenty already had Ulster under-21 and two Ulster minor and two All-Ireland colleges medals. His father, Tommy, captained Derry to All-Ireland minor success in 1965 and under-21 success in 1968.

Dermot McNicholl from Glenullin had been the captain of the 1983 All-Ireland minor championship winning side, winning three Ulster minor and three Ulster under-21 championship medals. He made his senior debut in 1983, having won three Sigerson Cup medals with Queen's, captained Glenullin to a remarkable 1985 county championship victory, went out to Australia to play with the Melbourne club's development squad, and was Derry's star in the 1987 championship when an injury badly affected him in the All-Ireland semi-final against Meath. Again in 1993 injury affected him, keeping him out of the All-Ireland semi-final against Dublin, but he came on as a substitute.

Brian McCormick was another of the Lavey All-Ireland club medallists. Just twenty, 6 feet 2 in height and 14 stone in weight, he had won two Hogan medals with St Patrick's, Maghera, and Ulster minor and under-21 medals with Derry, as well as Ulster and All-Ireland club medals with Lavey.

A student, Declan Bateson from Ballinderry was 5 feet 9, weighed 11 stone, and won Ulster and All-Ireland medals in 1989 with Derry minors and won a 1992 National League medal.

Stephen Mulvenna from St Mary's, Faughanvale, was twenty-eight, stood 5 feet 11, and weighed 13 stone. He won a Railway Cup medal in 1987, having started his career with Antrim.

Richard Ferris of Drumsurn was thirty, stood 5 feet 7, weighed 11 stone, and had made his second return to the panel in 1993 when he scored one of the match-winning goals against Down in the Ulster championship. Another was scored by Éamonn Burns of Ballinascreen, who stood 6 feet 1, weighed 13 stone, and at the age of twenty-one had already been unfortunate to miss two seasons through injury.

Of the many strongholds of Gaelic Derry one could choose to illustrate the resilience of the community, Lavey just happens to be the most successful. It does not appear on any signposts or maps, but Lavey is a proud place. Since winning the All-Ireland club championship in 1991, the parish bulletin has proclaimed: "St Mary's, Lavey, Ireland's premier parish." There are under two thousand people here in St Mary's parish, spread in two townlands, Gulladuff and Mayogall.

Knoughloughtrim, the bay of Maghera and Culnady all serve as homes to people who consider themselves residents of Londonderry. The GAA was the people of Lavey's way of expressing their communal identity.

The McGurks grew up within a decent kick-out from the Erin's Own playing field. Back in 1933 Anthony McGurk helped found the club. Anthony's sons Anthony Joe and Hugh became useful footballers and hurlers in the mid-1940s. Hugh was always encouraging his own sons to play football. There were eight boys and five girls in the family, and few suspected that the pedigree would be so rewarding. Anthony, now forty-four and living in Derry, where he is head civil engineer for Derry City Council, won All-Star award in both attack and defence, captained Derry to the 1976 Ulster title, and won an All-Ireland under-21 medal alongside Éamonn Coleman in 1968. He still lines out occasionally at full-forward for Lavey, playing a week before younger brother John won his 1993 All-Ireland medal. Joe, who is thirty-nine, played more hurling than football, winning two All-Ireland junior hurling medals and coaching the famous 1986 under-21 hurlers who beat Antrim and 1990 minors who won an Ulster title. Martin (thirty-four), Séamus (thirty-three), Paddy (twenty-nine), John (twenty-seven), Colm (twenty-six), and Ciarán (twenty-five). Of the girls, Aileen played for Derry, scoring two goals in the 1978 All-Ireland junior final, and the other four played for Lavey. It was while watching five of his sons play for Lavey one day in 1992 that Hugh McGurk died from a heart attack.

St Patrick's Day, 1991, was the greatest day in the history

of St Mary's parish. "The big factor", Brendan Convery confirmed amid the smell of sweat and embrocation in the Croke Park dressing-room, "was that they were playing for their parish and would not hear of defeat." "We are a very tight area," says Johnny McGurk. "Our most bitter rival is not Donegal, Dublin, or Cork. It is Bellaghy."

Brendan Regan made a breath-taking save. Brian McCormack was set up by Séamus Downey and Colm McGurk for the winning goal eight minutes after half time, which gave Lavey a 2-5 to 0-4 lead. Every one of the sixteen. Six of eight McGurk brothers started on the team; a seventh, Anthony, now forty-three and the winner of an All-Star award in 1972, replaced his brother Colm for the last few minutes.

Tony Regan, manager of beaten finalists Salthill, complimented their spirit: "They never gave us time to settle." While the boys gave a raucous version of "I Wish I Was Back Home in Derry" inside, team captain John McGurk begged the gateman to let him back on the field, "just to stand on it one more time." He still maintains that "the club championship was the best day of my life until the All-Ireland in 1993. There is nothing like captaining your club team to win an All-Ireland. Absolutely nothing, because you grow up with your club team. It is the same people that you are meeting year in, year out, that you are talking to and playing with. That was something special."

The Lavey team was confined to eight families: Brendan Regan, Damien Doherty, Anthony Scullion, Brian Scullion, John McGurk, Henry Downey, Ciarán McGurk; Damien O'Boyle, James Chivers 0-1, Fergal Rafferty, Brian

McCormack 1-6, Hugh Martin McGurk 0-1, Don
Mulholland, Séamus Downey, Colm McGurk. Substitute:
Anthony McGurk for Colm McGurk.

Éamonn McCann wrote in the aftermath of Derry's All-
Ireland semi-final victory: "This may provide an explanation
for the rootedness of the GAA in rural areas and its strange
seeming irrelevance in Derry city. Nationalists in the city,
for all their widely canvassed grievances, lived in a solid
mass, self sufficient as far as identity was concerned. They
have never needed the GAA the way Lavey has, where it's a
moot point whether the GAA is part of the community or
the community is part of the GAA."

"Lavey came through really out of the blue," Henry
Downey says. "Derry football was certainly not on a high at
that time. And here you had a very small rural parish
coming through and taking an All-Ireland crown. It
certainly did a lot for Gaelic football at the minute. A lot of
clubs sat up and took notice and felt if Lavey can do that,
why can't we do it? We know these fellows, we play with
these fellows, the rest of Derry can do it too. It helped. It is
not solely responsible for Derry's turnaround, but the 1993
All-Ireland was like doing a Lavey over again."

What is this place called Derry? The county is a redundant
administrative unit, preserved nowadays by the GAA
almost alone as the British government recognises new
boundaries between Derry, Magherafelt, Limavady,
Coleraine and even part of Cookstown districts. But it takes
more than a bureaucrat's bidding to eradicate a county.

Derry's landscape has long shaped the character of its

people: bounded clearly by the broad Atlantic to the north, the Bann, the second-greatest river in Ireland in terms of catchment area, to the east, the Sperrins and Slieve Gallion to the south, and the Foyle, Ireland's eighth-longest river and a highway to the great world beyond, to the west.

At 523,000 acres it is in the middle range of Irish counties, Ulster's fifth and Ireland's fifteenth-largest, slightly smaller than Meath or England's Nottinghamshire, and slightly larger than Kilkenny or Wicklow. It is the fifth most densely populated county in Ireland.

Churchmen drew up Derry's first boundaries. When they sat down at the Synod of Ráth Bhreasail in 1111 to define the territory without the benefit of maps or demarcation lines in the heavily wooded countryside, they allocated a stretch of territory from the Finn valley all the way down to Lough Derg to the mouth of the River Roe to the Cinéal Eoghain diocese, with its see in Raphoe and Derry. While other dioceses of the twelfth century, notably Ardstraw (incorporated in Derry in 1240) and Ráth Luraigh (transferred from Maghera to Derry in 1247) failed to last the pace, both Raphoe and Derry survived, and at the synod of 1320 the bishop of Derry was allocated all of Inishowen, east Tyrone as far as Castlederg, and the east bank of the Bann as far as Bellaghy. It is an ecclesiastical boundary that has survived to this day, while the Church of Ireland reverted to the joint Raphoe and Derry diocese after 1834.

The new settlers of the seventeenth century created new territorial divisions under English law. Derry was incorporated as a city for nine years from 1604. The shire of

Coleraine they had created in 1603 was replaced with the new and foreign-sounding London-Derry in 1613. Port-stewart and part of the east bank of the Bann were transferred from Antrim, and all the land from Maghera to Lough Neagh transferred from Tyrone, losing to the Red Hand county the breeding ground of future All-Ireland footballers: Ballinascreen, Bellaghy, and Magherafelt. Derry, Limavady and Coleraine were given parliamentary representation in the Irish parliament.

It is no accident that the modern city of Derry can be seen from the reconstructed Grianán of Aileach, a few miles away in County Donegal. While spiritually the high kings were allocated Tara in the territory of Liam Hayes in Breagha Laoire, the actual power of high-kingship, exactor of tributes from seven of the nine kingdoms of Ireland, was with the Cinéal Eoghain and the Northern Uí Néill.

Derry's Gaels of a score of generations ago knew their place in the hierarchical, structured society of ancient Ireland: at or near the top. They paid poets and genealogists to antedate their lineage back to Eoghan, son of Niall Naoi-Ghiallach, Niall of the Nine Hostages, a legendary figure even in the fifth century when the over-kingdom of Eamhain Mhacha collapsed. Then this Cinéal Eoghain of Aileach arranged to share the high-kingship of Ireland, firstly with their Ó Néill cousins the Cinéal Chonaill and then with the Clann Cholmáin of Mí.

Between the years 507 and 980 some sixteen of Ireland's forty-three high kings came from Aileach. Their names don't feature on many birth certificates nowadays:

Eoghan's supposed grandson Muireartach mac Earc, three of his sons, Fearghas, Dónall Ilchealgach and Baothán, Dónall's sons Eochaidh and Aodh Allan Uairidhneach, Baothán's son Colmán Rimhidh, Colmán's second cousin Suibhne Meann mac Fhiachna, Aodh Uairidhneach's great-grandson Fearghal mac Mhaoldúin, and his sons Aodh Allan, who established the primacy of Armagh, and Niall Frosach, who abdicated in 770 to enter Iona monastery.

Niall's son Aodh "Ingir" Oirní became one of the most notorious of the Aileach kings, extending the Derry-Iona influence into Kells but earning a formal curse pronounced by the clergy at Tara because he was implicated in the death of the abbot of Raphoe. He died fighting in Louth. His brother Aodh Finnliath and his son Niall Caille, who drove the Vikings from Derry in 833, carried on the tradition. Aodh's son Niall Glúndubh, "of the black knee," attempted to pre-empt Brian Bóramha. Having shown his sporting interests by reviving the Aonach Tailteann, this great warrior-king reigned for just three eventful years, 916 to 919, during which he organised a drive to rid the country of the Vikings. He laid siege to Raghnall in the Viking city of Waterford in the summer of 917. He gathered a massive army to rid the country of the Norse, and met his death at the apocalyptic battle of Islandbridge fighting the Dublin Vikings, 15 September 919. The king of Ulster, the king of Breagha and the king of Oirialla perished alongside him. The last Cinéal Eoghain high king was Niall Glúndubh's grandson, Dónall Ó Néill, high king from 956 to 980, who arranged to have his naval fleet dragged over the Fews Mountains in Armagh to Lough Ennel and garrisoned rebellious districts in Meath. He died of politeness, so anxious not to cause offence by going to the toilet during a harp recital in Armagh that his bladder burst. Most of these Derry-Donegal kings were buried in splendour at Armagh, Aodh Allan mac Fhearghail in Clonmacnoise and Niall Glúndubh at Colm Cille's monastery in Kells.

In the chaos that followed the death of Brian Bóramha, Dónall and Muireartach mac Lochlainn both fought for the high-kingship, but in a period characterised more by draws and replays than outright victories, they reached a stalemate with the Uí Briain and Uí Conchúir, and the last king of Aileach was killed by William le Petit in Meath in 1185. Today McLoughlin is the second most common surname in Derry, behind O'Doherty and ahead of Kelly, Bradley, Brown, and McCloskey.

One of Muireartach's colleagues was Eachmharcach Ó Catháin, and his family were to emerge from the Laggan district of east Donegal to take a large tract of territory around Coleraine and Kennaght. Their last chief, Dónall, was summoned with Aodh Ó Néill to London. Ó Néill fled to Rome, Ó Catháin went and died in the Tower of London in 1628; there are many Kanes in Coleraine to this day, and McCloskey and McAvinney are offshoots from this Cinéal Eoghain branch.

Only fragments of the story of the Celtic past of the north-west survive, but its relevance remains strong. Politician John Hume referred to the dexterity of these remote predecessors in his inaugural speech in London's House of

Commons, when he reminded the members for British boroughs who legislate for Ireland how sixth-century Ulster people were able to pay tribute to the kings of Ireland and Argyll at the same time.

The name of Niall Glúndubh, who had died in glorious failure trying to free Ireland of the Viking scourge, was evoked in the surname adopted by the most successful Cinéal Eoghain family. From 1230 onwards they used the name of the warrior king in all its martial glory, Ó Néill, as they built up a powerful base in the north-west. They were based in Tyrone, but the Foyle and Derry was their seaport. When the concept of kingdom-nations arrived in Britain and Ireland from the Continent in the sixteenth century, it was the Uí Néill who declared the revival of the Irish kingdom and organised European help.

And beside the Red Hand and the doomed attempts of Conn, Seán, Aodh Rua and Eoghan to carry on Niall's tradition was the gentler story of Colm Cille and his cell in the oak groves. Michael O'Clery's annals recorded the headlines of ancient Derry's history under Ó Néill, Mac Lochlainn and Ó Dochartaigh patronage: the wonder-tales of St Colm Cille, born of royal Cinéal Eoghain blood and founder of an ecclesiastical empire that bridged the North Channel, Niall Caille's defeat of the Vikings in Derry, Dónall Mac Lochlainn's death there in 1121, the power and glory of the mediaeval diocese where abbot Giolla Mac Liaigh was consecrated archbishop of Armagh in 1137, Flaitheartach Ó Brolcháin's compulsory purchase order on eighty houses to build his monastic enclosure in 1162, his doorway and limekiln, and eventually destruction: the panic of de Courcy's arrival in February 1197, followed by the invasion and destruction of Thomas fitz Roland in 1212 or 1214.

Unlike de Courcy, the new invaders of the sixteenth century were colonists on a quasi-religious crusade, this time prepared to ignore the rules of war. For colonists war was a mission, not a sport.

Derry lay at a key point in the invaders' campaign to outwit Seán Ó Néill. Edward Randolph sailed in from Bristol in September 1566 and lasted two months before he was killed. His garrison stayed on, stockpiling their ammunition in the ancient cathedral. When someone accidentally sparked it off on 21 April 1567, the cathedral and a large part of both garrison and town were blown to kingdom come. The survivors were evacuated and went to more hospitable climes in Carrickfergus.

The Uí Néill eventually succumbed when Aodh Rua's army was devastated at Kinsale, and greedy eyes were turned on his vast estates in Ulster. Their Derry allies supported them to the end. Feidhlimí Ó Dochartaigh had signed a treaty with a French envoy in 1550 alongside Conn Bacach Ó Néill. Sir Cahir O'Doherty staged the last revolt in Derry, in 1608. His rebellion lasted just two more months before his death at Kilmacrenan, Co Donegal, and the swordsmen who sailed from Derry in 1609 were among the last of the Gaelic armies to leave the country.

The conflict that followed was slow and unrelenting, between cultures, between religions, between legal systems and even between place-names: Derry and Londonderry,

Ballinascreen and Draperstown, Muff and Eglington. The destruction of large amounts of their records and literature did not deny the inhabitants of Derry their sense of place.

The Londonderry charter of 13 March 1613 was designed to wipe the ancient name from the map for all time. The new Anglican cathedral was built on the site of the ancient Catholic one between 1628 and 1633.

The number of Protestants supposedly massacred in Derry when the dispossessed rebelled in 1641 runs to four times the Protestant population of the county; and the survivors of the massacre seemed numerous enough to carry on unaffected throughout the 1640s. By seventeenth-century standards the events of 1641 and 1649 were unremarkable. Two-thirds of the population died in the famine that followed the war, unenlightened by political or religious martyrdom. But even so the mythology is so strong that gasps could be heard when historian Brendan Bradshaw calculated that more Catholics died in 1641 than supposed victims. Like the Pope offering Te Deums to be sung in gratitude for King William's victory at the Boyne, it fits uneasily on the mythology.

The nickname Maiden City was earned in two sieges, the longer one near-forgotten, the shorter one the instrument of propaganda and sectarian triumphalism. The first siege, when Ulster Scots under Lord Montgomery and Robert Stewart attempted to take the city from April to August 1649, was raised by Eoghan Rua Ó Néill. The 1688–89 siege was a skirmish in comparison. The gates were shut on 7 December, but the siege did not begin until after the Battle of Claudy in April and lasted just two months. The difference with the second siege was propaganda. Within months George Walker's *True Account of the Siege of Londonderry* appeared, followed by John Mackenzie's contradictory *Narrative of the Siege of Londonderry* a year later. While Anglicans and Presbyterians bickered about the heroism of the defenders, the Jacobite story was never told.

The new name of the city served as an exercise in triumphalism. When Derry City Council changed the name back in the 1980s their move was blocked, and the British authorities told them they only had the authority to change the name of the council itself, not the city. There are legions of anecdotes of undelivered letters and unconnected telephone calls because they have not used the epithet of Londonderry.

The sectarian origins of Londonderry could not be avoided. When the Catholic Board of 1814 was being suppressed by the British government, the Apprentice Boys club was formed. George Dawson's speech in favour of Catholic emancipation was made at the Walker memorial in 1828. John Mitchel, born near Dungiven in 1815, became a leader of the Young Ireland movement. Sectarian rioting broke out in April 1869, and the town police force was abolished in favour of the RIC a year later.

Like so many Derry emigrants, the town itself begat its progeny abroad. Derry in Rockingham County, New Hampshire, is best known as the place where Robert Frost once lived. Famous for horse racing, it was named after Derry in 1827 (it even has a companion Londonderry) and has a population of 13,000. Derry in Pennsylvania is a satellite of Pittsburgh with 3,000 residents, while a small town on the Rio Grande about 100 miles east of El Paso is also known as Derry. Coleraine in Minnesota has a population of about 1,000. There is also Coleraine in South Australia and Coleraine in Québec province.

In 1920 Derry found itself a hostage city, on the wrong side of the new border that divided Ireland. Illegal and quasi-legal unionist armed forces roamed the streets. When a Catholic majority was elected to the city council in 1920, fourteen Catholics and four Protestants were killed in disturbances. The Boundary Commission inexplicably failed to return Derry to its hinterland. The city council was abolished and the infamous Derrymander imposed. By 1966 there were 20,126 Catholics and 10,274 Protestants, yet the council was still unionist-controlled. In the south ward 10,047 Catholics and 1,138 Protestants elected eight nationalist councillors; in the north ward 2,530 Catholics and 3,946 Protestants elected eight unionist councillors; and in the Waterside ward 1,852 Catholics and 3,697 Protestants elected four unionist councillors. The Derrymander was so notorious that the corporation was abolished as the first move by Terence O'Neill to reform Northern Ireland's sectarian election laws in November 1968.

Passions ran high. In November 1924 Éamon de Valera was imprisoned for a month for speaking in favour of a Sinn Féin candidate at an election. Of 206 non-manual government employees in Derry in 1951, just 16 were Catholics.

Derry was resented and discriminated against by its own provincial government. Unemployment ran to double the average for the province. It did enjoy wartime prosperity when Derry became a base for the US Atlantic fleet in February 1942. The 1965 decision, under Unionist pressure, to downgrade Magee, the city's third-level college, and establish the province's second university in the Protestant town of Coleraine was the final affront.

After October 1968, when Derry Citizens' Action Committee was formed and the RUC attack on civil rights marchers in 1968 caused worldwide protest, Derry became famous round the world. Samuel Devenny was beaten to death by the RUC, the first of hundreds of Derry people to die in the conflict. Magherafelt, Burntollet, Creggan and the Bogside became synonymous with tragedy and heartbreak. It was nice that Lavey, Glenullin and Newbridge should push them out of the headlines for a few weeks at least.

Considering that the arrival of large numbers of uninvited guests is the recipe for tragedy all over the world, Derry people have been surprisingly fraternal for the past 385 years. Although some of the Londonderry people saw the civil rights campaign as gains for the Derry people at their expense, years of living in close quarters has taught them that co-operation and good humour can cut through the bitterness. Not for them the pogroms of Belfast and the sectarian rioting that erupted every decade since the 1980s.

Nowadays Derry City Council shares power. Local politics is dominated by constitutional nationalism; John Hume, as an elder statesman of the SDLP, was once tipped as a president of the European Parliament. In the city Sinn Féin's Martin McGuinness is matched by Gregory

Campbell of the Democratic Unionist Party. In the county William Ross is the latest in a long line of traditional, dependable Official Unionist MPs.

Some of Cahir O'Doherty's gallowglasses or Derry's seventeenth-century planted guests may have brought the game of camànachd with them from Scotland. The two great scholars of pre-GAA hurling, Liam Ó Caithnia and Art Ó Maolfabhail, concur that hurling is an ancient game, with a plethora of references in Brehon law, mediaeval sagas, folk songs, and later newspaper accounts. They also believe that it came in two varieties, a broad-boss "báire" played in Leinster and Munster and a narrow-boss "camán" ground-hurling played in the north. The northern tradition was seriously disadvantaged by the Michael Cusack rules of hurling drawn up in 1883, with their heavy Munster, Leinster and Galway bias, but, barred on class grounds from participation in the TCD-originated game of hurley, it had little choice but to conform to the new GAA rules.

In 1837 an Ordnance Survey officer, Col. Colby, commented how scrupulously the people of Derry kept the sabbath and had no public pastimes. But Colby had missed the sound of ash and sally as the winter matches of "cammon" took place. Derry and its hinterland in Burt, twelve miles from the city, was once a stronghold of the ground game and perhaps had a hurling code of its own. It appears to have been interdenominational, with Presbyterian Scottish settlers importing the ancestor of modern shinty, camànachd, to Derry with them. Gaelic areas also preserved their game. A folk song records a game between Ballinascreen and Dungiven at Mark Cromie's field on 17 January 1825, when the referee had some fingers removed by over-enthusiastic players before he managed to throw in the ball:

> The discourse passed among them along the highway,
> Saying, Boys, I am afraid we will not get fair play,
> But they were mistaken for we let them know,
> Though bred in the mountain we knew what to do.
> We played them with justice and that I'll maintain,
> We gave them no reason on us to complain.

The one-armed hurling recorded in Burt may have been unique in Ireland. Ó Caithnia gathered recollections gathered in turn by Paddy MacNamee of how the hurling ball was known as a nag, niug, or neag, and played in Burt in the lifetime of the uncle of one of his sources, around 1846. According to the Dungiven balladeer, Francie Pheadair "gave the cnag the first boise" in that 1825 "commons" match. MacNamee's sources described how sally hurls were used, the ball was known as a nag or boule, the bas was known as a blade (slightly larger than a hockey stick), and the turn known as a bucht: "the camon had a nice bucht" (a corruption of *beacht*). The feet were used to usher the ball along the ground. A local man, Thomas McCafferty, who lived around 1880 recalled terms such as cowping and kepping the boule—guarding the ball from opponents. Another local, James Whorriskey, described how sally roots or stumps were shaped and a bucht, or curve, put on them, leaving a four-foot-long stick that resembled a shinty stick. When the GAA arrived, Burt allowed both the old narrow-bas and the new wide-bas hurls on their team.

On Derry's Waterside, MacNamee was told, Ballyowen and Cill Fhionnáin would play each Christmas Day. "Until sixty or seventy years ago camán was the only sport for Gaels of Derry," then county chairman Paddy Larkin wrote in the *Irish Press* supplement for the Golden Jubilee of the GAA in 1934. He recalled that pre-GAA goals were eight miles apart, and reckoned that the decline of hurling began about 1870.

Antrim's influence could be felt on the east. Jeanne Cooper Foster's 1951 *Ulster Folklore* comments that beaches were favourite pitches for Christmas hurling matches in Magilligan. In Portrush and Bushmills in 1874 it was reported that football was played only by British soldiers, and cammon was the only game played around Burt. The cammon was played at Christmas.

The memory of the narrow-bladed wide-soled camán was evoked again in the 1950s, and GAA president J. J. Stuart stated that there was a hurling club once in every parish in Derry. But the GAA had failed in its task of reviving this Derry hurling. Why and how, we can only speculate.

But the hurling lore had led to the neglect of what may have been a strong football tradition. Francis McBride from Temple Maol near Ballinascreen was sixty-five when he told folklorist Michael Murphy in 1950 of football in the six towns: "In my young days a great football match was played every so often between Muinameal and Aghasruba. One would send a Ban-tha to the other. That was a challenge. Muinameal slept late. Aghasruba rose early, McGurk the basket-maker, a great kicker, sent this bantha to McAleer in Muinameal. For the late sleepers to come over on a certain Sunday and kick the early risers."

They learnt their football early in Ballinascreen.

3

SLOW STARTERS
1884–1947

Both football and hurling were organised in the burst of GAA activity that followed the association's launch in the four years after 1884, Cusack's "prairie fire." A letter of support at the inaugural meeting of the GAA in Thurles was read from a Mr McLaughlin in Derry, father of a later county board chairman. St Patrick's, Waterside, was said to have been founded in advance of the association in October 1884, possibly by Mr McLaughlin, according to a later edition of the *Derry People*. Magherafelt had a club within two months of the association's foundation in November 1884. By June 1885 Desertmartin had a branch of the new association. It was claimed fifty years later that Ballinascreen and Dunamore in County Tyrone were the first two clubs in south Derry.

Hurling competed for the attention of young athletes with Londonderry and Foyle Rugby Clubs, Derry and Lower Cumber Cricket Clubs, Bann Rowing Club, City of Derry Lacrosse Club, St Columb's Court, and dozens of soccer clubs. As early as 1884 North and South Derry were regarded as separate divisions for the Irish Football Association cup competition. There was also the spectacle of the aristocracy playing with Derry Polo Club. Derry had three clubs in 1887, and the *Freeman's Journal* weekly sports paper, *Sport,* referred to "great activity under the walls of

Derry" in a report that St Patrick's, Waterside, were playing
football and hurling matches against other long-forgotten
Derry city clubs with beautifully expressive names:
Hibernians, Emeralds, Sunburst, and Young Ireland. They
also travelled regularly to play Claudy and into Donegal to
play Buncrana Emmets, Newtowncunningham, Cahirhoo
and Burt, already noted as skilled wielders of the camán.

Brendan Behan would have been pleased to find so many
splits on the agenda of the early GAA in Derry, with
contradictory sets of officers—often including the same
people—being elected. For example, Patrick Campbell, a
clerk from Bright Stars Club in Derry city, was elected
secretary of the county board in September 1888, deposed
eight weeks later, re-elected in December, re-elected in 1889,
and deposed in 1890. Representatives of six clubs—Burt,
Waterside St Patrick's, Hibernians, Emeralds, Éire Óg, and St
Columb's—reported to the Derry convention at the Éire Óg
committee rooms on 28 October 1888. James Doherty, a
butcher from Bright Stars, was elected president, Daniel
Farren treasurer, and Edward McGeoghegan secretary;
Charles Doherty, James Carlin, William Barr, John
Concannon, James McCallion, Joseph McLaughlin, John
Friel, Francis Martin. A month earlier a Derry county board
was formed, with Patrick Bradley, a stonemason connected
with St Patrick's in Waterside, as chairman, Campbell as
secretary, Doherty as treasurer, and committee members
Charles McGrory, a coach-builder, Charlie McDermott, a
labourer, George McLaughlin, a labourer from Claudy,
Bernard McElhinney, a farmer from Portlough, and Edward
Hasson, a dealer from Foreglen. These officers were

eventually re-installed in September 1890 for the third time in two years. The Waterside club officers elected on 25 February 1888 were J. E. O'Doherty, William Carlin, Francis Carlin, John Reigh, Peter Bradley, Joseph Doherty, John Heaney, D. Heaney, P. Clare, J. W. McBey, P. Doherty, D. McFeeley, Richard Magill, and M. McCrystal. Eugene Colhoun was elected club secretary the following year.

In November 1888 the State Papers in Dublin Castle record: "There is no doubt that the GAA is becoming an important body throughout this northern division. Twelve months ago there was one county here in which it had anything like a footing. Now it is pretty firmly established in six counties, the only ones in which it is not established being Antrim, Donegal, and Tyrone." In December 1888 Derry was one of only eight counties to have paid affiliation fees to the Central Council.

Despite the GAA president Maurice Davin's telling the 1889 congress that there were not enough clubs in Derry to justify the foundation of a county board, there were fourteen clubs in action, two from Derry, three from Donegal, and nine from Derry city: John Mitchels of Claudy, O'Briens of Muldonagh, Burt Hibernians, Killea Hibernians, Portlough Harps, St Patrick's of Waterside, St Columb's, Hibernians, Emeralds, McCarthys, Éire Óg, Bright Stars, Sunburst, and Erin's Hopes. John Mullan of Claudy, James McLaughlin, Michael Devine from Muldonagh, Denis Kerlin, William Hennish and Patrick O'Kane were organising the GAA in the county. The Derry city clubs especially seemed to come and go at will: different sources list totals of eight and sixteen clubs in Derry in 1890.

The *Derry Journal* records the early activity: Strabane against Waterside in Lifford, Waterside against Burt in Burt, where they were met by "the king and his followers." Elaborate two-hour matches involving an hour of hurling and an hour of football. The arrival of Emmets from Dundalk on 10 June 1888 to play Derry Hibernians in Rosemount before three thousand spectators, followed by a baton charge on the Sarsfields Flute Band from Rosemount for defying a ban on their playing anywhere except on the field. Sentences of one to six months were imposed on eighteen people after the disorder. Hibernians players' names were recorded: John O'Kane, Philip Mullan, John Harvey, William Dillon, Patrick Doyle, Daniel McFeeley, Neil Canning, Charles O'Hagan, Anthony McGranaghan, John Anderson, John McKay, Festus Whelan, John O'Neill, Andrew McQuigg, John Phelan, Patrick Doherty, George Lynch, Hugh Friel, James McGee, John Lynch, and John MacMahon.

Waterside visited Claudy on 18 September 1888 on ten outside cars. The GAA staged a Christmas Day tournament in 1888 to raise money for a national monument fund. Waterside went to Dundalk to play Dundalk Faughs on 19 January 1889. Among a two thousand attendance an Irish National Foresters GAA excursion to Dundalk in June 1890 included the RIC spies, who noted that although IRB men from Derry and Dundalk mingled there was no meeting of the IRB. Such songs as "The Wearing of the Green", "The Boys of Wexford" and "The Boys of '98" were sung, and three cheers were raised for the Phoenix Park Invincibles. In July 1890 St Patrick's of Derry played a challenge match against St Patrick's of Dublin and were entertained at Clonturk House by the Dublin county committee. The Derry men wore puce jerseys and white knickers, and were greatly hampered by the habit of stopping the ball with their feet.

In 1889 a county hurling championship was won by Hibernians from Derry city. Waterside St Patrick's were recorded as 1891 county hurling champions, having beaten Hibernians by 1-4 to 0-1. The elaborate cup with which they were presented was uncovered in the Waterside parochial house by a local monsignor, Austin Duffy, during the GAA's centenary year in 1984. It was unlikely that the cup could have been easily retrieved for competition from such a home: in November 1891 the new Bishop of Derry, John Keys O'Doherty, came out against any games being played on Sundays. It effectively finished the early burst of GAA activity in Derry.

It was probably the foundation of the Gaelic League that was to help nurse Derry back to health. Around 1900 nationalist Ireland reorganised. Catholic clergy became heavily involved in the organisation of cultural and sporting interests for their flock. The Gaelic League developed rapidly in the north-west, as did the United Irish League, the Ancient Order of Hibernians, the Irish National Foresters, feiseanna, and a plethora of pipe bands, many of which were to accompany Derry hurling teams wherever they went. In 1902 Seán an Díomais from Belfast came from Derry to play a challenge hurling match. Burt, St Patrick's, Derry Hibernians and St Columb's were already back in action. An Easter tournament on 18 April 1903, with Limavady, Éire

Óg, Cumann na nGael, St Patrick's, Sarsfields, and Cumann Liteartha na Gaedhilge, all marching in their colours with their hurleys, Foresters in full regalia, pipe bands, and a giant banner saying *We shall rise again* energised the games in Derry city once more. On 18 October the message came from the Bishop's House once more: "Reverend sirs, I was surprised to see lately in the local papers notice of hurling matches being played in the suburbs of the city. Those taking part in these games cannot be ignorant that sports of this description on Sundays were disapproved of many years ago and were then discontinued in obedience to my wishes. I regret to find that an attempt to renew them is now being made, in that our young men are showing a forgetfulness of the sanctity of the Lord's day. We are commanded by God himself to keep that day holy and few will say that this commandment is fulfilled by playing hurley, football, or any other athletic game. I call on our young men to desist from these unseemly exhibitions on Sundays and to show for the future that they are animated by the spirit of true Catholics by keeping holy the Lord's day as they are commanded to do."

Whether puritanism or fear of radical politics motivated the bishop we never shall know. But when it came to inter-county competition, Derry GAA faced an equally puritanical opposition. Trains rather than training were the cause of the isolation of these early hurlers from Derry city. It was virtually impossible to get the Great Northern Railway to run an excursion on a Sunday. In their splendid isolation, Derry were able to call on one of the best hurling squads in Ulster.

Twice those knickerbocker hurlers made it to the All-Ireland semi-final. In the 1901 Ulster hurling final on 5 April 1903 Antrim Lámh Dhearg beat Derry St Patrick's by 41 points to 12 points, but the following year Derry beat the new Lámh Dhearg club from Strabane by 6-13 to 0-1 in Strabane, and Antrim by 2-7 to 2-5 in a final played on 11 October 1903, the day of the bishop's anti-hurling missive. The venue was Celtic Park, Belfast, and the match was listed as "for the 1902 Ulster senior hurling championship."

The Gaelic League was active in starting hurling clubs wherever they had Irish-language and literary classes, and its influence is clear in the north-west hurling league, which brought together teams from three counties that winter: Cumann Liteartha na Gaedhilge, Cumann na nGael, St Patrick's, Éire Óg, Burt Hibernians, Limavady, Sarsfields, and Strabane Lámh Dhearg. None of the memoirs of these Derry teams were ever recorded, but the father of long-time Derry chairman Tommy Mellon was one of the team. Many of those pioneer hurlers must have lived until the 1970s, and they live on in photographs, tense young men clutching hurleys, four of them with Edwardian moustaches, or as a list of initialled surnames on yellowing newsprint: A. Cowley (Éire Óg), P. Bonnar (Sarsfields), D. McLoughlin (captain, Sarsfields), J. L. Elliot (St Patrick's), Thomas Mellon (Éire Óg), Patrick McCallin (Éire Óg), John McCallin (Sarsfields), M. Cannon (Sarsfields), Hugh Coyle (Sarsfields), Andrew Coyle (Sarsfields), Daniel Coyle (Sarsfields), H. Brown (Sarsfields), Peter McCallin (Éire Óg), J. Duffy (Éire Óg), Henry Patton

(Limavady), James Crossan (St Patrick's), and P. Heaney (St Patrick's).

Derry had to travel all night on their journey to Drogheda to meet Dublin in the All-Ireland semi-final on 5 June 1904, because there was no suitable train from the GNR: the railway board objected to football teams using their trains for Sunday games, on religious grounds.

The final score, Dublin 6-17, Derry 0-6, reflected the difference between the teams, Dublin having led by 3-12 to nil at half time. Derry lined out in white jerseys with a green shamrock, and brought a formidable contingent of pipers with them on the journey. "The ground was not suitable for either team, but for hurling it was absolutely dangerous," according to the *Freeman's Journal,* and Derry were sorely hampered by the length of the grass, as "Derry play mostly on the ground." Their aerial play was defective and their dribbling a complete failure. Derry still managed to score six points in the second half after trailing 3-12 to nil at half time.

The *Freeman's Journal* continued: "The details were looked after by the secretary and several of the central, Leinster, Dublin and Louth councils. Mr John C. O'Brien refereed impartially. The arrangements, with the exception of the long grass, were passable, and it seems strange that provincial teams should have been asked to play on such a meadow. There was a good attendance but it was not at all a remunerative one, the gaps being numerous.

"The hurling was the first item and the teams were on the line on time, the Derrymen having the sun at their backs, the Metropolitans attired mostly in the Faugh colours while Derry played in white sweaters adorned with green shamrock. It was soon apparent that the Dubliners were the more expert and points were registered in rapid succession. The Derry backs fought hard but were unable to resist the attacks made upon them, in which they were sorely hampered by the grass. The cúl báire saved repeatedly in good style, and were it not for his exertion the total of major scores would have been considerable. Still the score mounted up, Derry making two ineffectual incursions into Dublin territory. The Derry play was ruined by the ground, their aerial play being most effective while their dribbling was a failure. It would have mattered little, however, and Dublin led at half time by three goals and 12 points to Derry's nil, Alan Keating and Harty of Faughs being conspicuous by hard work, the latter on the wing and the former in preventing Derry passing the half way mark. The resumption was opened by a perceptible easing off by Dublin and an awakening by Derry which resulted in their breaking the monotonous regularity of Dublin scoring by notching a point. They kept hammering away with praiseworthy fortitude and added two more minors which Dublin nullified by a goal. The Dublin team felt secure and did not over exert themselves, but while Derry added three more points they piled up three goals and five points, leaving the final record Dublin six goals and seventeen points, Derry six points."

Peter McCallin of Éire Óg was selected for Ulster's first inter-provincial hurling team in 1905.

Dublin were beaten by Cork in a replayed All-Ireland home final, 2-6 to 0-1, after a 1-7 draw in Tipperary, and

Cork finished a somewhat protracted All-Ireland series when they beat London by 3-13 to nil on a day on which their new athletic grounds were opened.

Railway, episcopal and foreign games difficulties may have combined to prevent Derry's putting in an appearance at the 1902 Croke Cup hurling semi-final on 16 October 1904 at Dundalk. The GNR refused to run an excursion for the 1902 Ulster final on 10 April of that year, so the final was fixed for Easter Monday. On one occasion, when the railway board discovered that a special train to run on a Sunday was for a football team, they cancelled it. Paddy Whelan of Newbliss, Ulster chairman, travelled to the Railway Commission hearings in London on 13 March 1908 to complain about the lack of facilities for GAA teams. Eventually a meeting between the GAA and the GNR board secured train facilities for teams on Sundays. It was alleged that the GNR had changed their Sunday train schedules specifically to prevent their being used by football teams.

A GAA revival was reported on 13 May 1905, and again in July 1913. Éire Óg, St Patrick's, Clann Uladh, Henry Grattans, Newtowncunningham Harps, John Mitchels from Claudy, Buncrana Emmets and Letterkenny Lámh Dhearg all resumed action. The championship teams were reduced from seventeen a side to thirteen a side to help clubs to field teams.

Burt Hibernians, who had played most of their early hurling in Derry, opted to represent Donegal in 1906; when they beat Antrim by 5-21 to 0-1 in the Ulster senior final on their home pitch they had twenty car loads, and cyclists came from Derry city to cheer them on. They also had the help of two extra players.

The Derry hurlers won the Ulster championship again in 1909, defeating Cavan by 2-8 to 0-2 in Clones and qualifying for a trip to the new GAA grounds in Jones's Road, Dublin, and a semi-final against a Kilkenny team represented by sixteen Mooncoin players and one from Erin's Own. J. J. Kenny, a colleague of Michael Cusack's in the 1880s revival of hurling, refereed. The match, played on 14 November, did not attract any of the media inquisitiveness of 1904 and was again fearsomely one-sided as Kilkenny won by 3-17 to 0-3, having led by 3-11 to nil at half time, and went on to beat Tipperary in the All-Ireland final.

The names of the team survive, testimony to their enthusiasm in the face of adversity: James Crossan, Peter McCallion, William Kelly, J. L. Elliot, E. Gallagher, Thomas Mellon, McRory, B. Doherty, John McCallion, P. Heaney, Thomas McCallion, Meenan, H. Elliot, M. Hampsey, D. Lynn, E. Coyle. Seven, including Thomas Mellon, had been in the 1903 team.

The team for the All-Ireland semi-final was: P. Cusack, J. Kelly, P. Elliot, J. Sidham, E. Gallagher, E. Miller, B. Doherty, J. McEvoy, J. McCullagh, F. McCullagh, P. Kenny, J. Mulvany, H. Elliott, D. Lynn, M. Hampsey (or Hensey), E. Coyle, W. McCullagh.

After the hurling championship of 1908, the game in Derry city came to an abrupt halt, and Waterside St Patrick's, winners of three early championships, vanished without trace. It may not be coincidental that the GAA's infamous ban on foreign games was in suspended animation between 1896 and 1902, allowing Derry city's

hurling clubs to resume activity. The ban was made
optional for county committees in 1903, but restored as a
compulsory ban in 1904. The same meeting of Derry GAA
board that suspended certain members for having played
foreign games also decided to postpone outstanding games.
British police, soldiers, sailors and militiamen were also
banned in 1902. But in Derry the Catholic clergy had
become involved in the establishment of soccer clubs,
perhaps to prevent their flocks being corrupted by the
dangers of proselytism, so that even at this stage soccer
clubs like St Columb's Court and a dozen junior clubs had
earned widespread support in the city.

The revival that the hurlers inspired was not going to die
away so easily, and soon there were inklings of a GAA
structure in the county. D. J. Murrin became a vice-
president of the GAA in the early 1900s. When the Ulster
Council was formed in March 1903, Derry's representative,
L. F. O'Kane, was elected secretary. O'Kane later held a
position on the Central Council, and J. McGovern was a
stalwart at Ulster Council meetings until the early 1920s.
Nevertheless, when Sarsfields won the revived hurling
championships in 1902 and 1903, Derry were included in
the draw for the 1902 football championship, but Tyrone
earned a walkover from Derry in a first-round tie fixed for
Dungannon. This was a good year for football in Ulster, as
Cavan beat Armagh in a final that took three meetings to
sort out and attracted a seven thousand attendance for the
second meeting of the teams.

In the draw for the 1904 championship, the first for

which all nine Ulster counties were included, Derry got a walkover from Donegal in a match fixed for 16 July, but there is no mention of their subsequent participation in the championship. Cavan may have beaten Derry, and a match that does not correspond to the draw is reported in the *Derry People* for 10 February 1906: Derry 1-3, Tyrone 0-2. Excursion trains were not the only problems the Ulster GAA faced from fundamentalist Protestants: Cookstown players and supporters were attacked by an Orange crowd of two hundred when they arrived to play Coalisland in a Tyrone club game.

In the confused circumstances of the time, Cavan are retrospectively accredited with a 1905 championship that may never have been played, and Derry enjoyed another walkover from Donegal in the 1906 championship, before travelling to Belfast on 18 August and a defeat of 1-14 to 0-4 at the hands of Antrim. The following year a match fixed between Derry and Donegal on 8 December in Letterkenny may have taken place, although neither team took subsequent part in the championship; it is unlikely in view of their relative strength at the time, but Derry were once said to have been due to play Monaghan in the 1907 Ulster final before the railway embargo put an end to their plans. The county had just seven affiliated clubs at this time, most of them city-based hurling teams. Tyrone were given a walkover by Derry in the 1910 championship, a match fixed for Dungannon on 8 May of that year. The death of Bishop Doherty in February 1907 and the succession of Charles McHugh the following September did not seem to help the GAA revive.

Handball has been played in the south Derry area at
least since the 1880s. In 1909 a South Derry and East
Tyrone league was organised in Dungannon and district.
Derry handballers competed in the Cookstown and district
league in 1911.

A revival of sorts took place on 22 July 1913 under
officials Séamus Mac Giolla and Hugh Casey. Ten clubs,
nine from the city and one from Buncrana, were organised.
An under-21 league was organised. Monaghan beat Derry
in the 1914 championship in the first championship
match to be played in Derry, before a crowd that paid a
total of £10 19s in threepences.

In the Ulster medal tournament of that year Derry
created a stir, reaching the final against Cavan before going
down by 1-3 to 0-2 on 31 May at Newbliss. Derry's first
football finalists were P. J. Casey (Clann Chonaill), J.
Canning (Sarsfields), John McKenna (Clann Chonaill), M.
Barr (Celtic), J. Meenan (Emmets), D. McCourt (Emmets), J.
McCloskey (St Patrick's), Hugh Casey (Clann Chonaill), S.
Brown (captain, Sarsfields), Joe Duffy (Volunteers), M. Rock
(Emmets), D. Doherty (Rapparees), A. Burke (Sarsfields),
John Doherty (Celtic), and V. Doherty (Clann Chonaill).

Grandiose claims were being made at GAA meetings
about the demise of soccer in Derry city. They may have
been premature, Derry soccer having been affected by the
after-effects of a 1912 split that tore the IFA apart and later
the suspension of competition during the First World War.
Anyway, the GAA in Derry was becoming side-tracked
itself. In March 1914 the Derry board had decided to allow
each club to make its own decision whether or not to

support the Irish Volunteers movement. In reality, Volunteer activity was reported to have brought Gaelic games to a halt by March 1915. Considering that most of the clubs were still Derry-based, it is unlikely that travel restrictions also prevented activity during 1915 and 1916, as was officially claimed. Derry county board was identified with the minority National Volunteers.

Nevertheless, Sarsfields beat Cavan Rory O'Mores by 2-0 to 0-1 in an Ulster club tournament organised for National Aid in 1916 but lost to Castleblayney Faughs by 2-5 to 2-1 in the Ulster final on 4 November 1916.

On 2 July 1916 Monaghan beat Derry at Clones in the Ulster quarter-final, and on 20 May 1917 Cavan beat Derry in Derry city.

The Brandywell grounds were recognised as one of the best in Ulster at this stage, with matches also played at Celtic Park and the Rosemount area; and among the more unusual matches they staged was the second replay of the 1919 Donegal county final, the eventual beaten finalists, Bundoran, having objected after defeats to Killygordon Red Hughs at two previous venues, Ballyshannon and Stranorlar. Five Donegal teams competed in the Derry and District League at this time.

On 28 April 1918 Antrim beat Derry by 4-1 to 2-4 at Celtic Park. Eventually, on 25 May 1919, Derry beat Fermanagh by 2-4 to 0-3 but were defeated by Antrim at the Brandywell by 1-4 to 1-1 on 1 June. St Columb's agreed to support an Ulster colleges competition in 1917. By 1918 Derry had eighteen clubs, including the imaginatively named Laburnum, and had a loan of £30 waived by the

Central Council in 1920. The five senior clubs were Emmets, Éire Óg, Celtic, Emerald Harps, and Caher O's from Buncrana.

Bernard McGlade had become the first Derry man to collect an All-Ireland medal in the meantime. Lavey man Bernard McGlade played with Caragh club in County Kildare and played alongside Larry Stanley on the 1919 team that won Kildare's second All-Ireland championship. His parents did not approve of his football activities, and he got his brother Charles, a dentist, to send a telegram saying he had a dental appointment. Using this as an excuse, Bernard went to Dublin for the final. He died in England in the late 1980s.

On 23 May 1920 Derry beat Donegal by 0-11 to 0-7 in Derry to reach the Ulster semi-final for the first time in their history. They were defeated by Cavan at Belturbet on 23 July; Cavan went on to win the Ulster tittle.

Political events delayed the 1920 championship until 13 November 1921, when Derry beat Donegal by 2-1 to 0-3 and followed up with a historic victory over Antrim four weeks later by 1-4 to 0-3 to reach their first Ulster final. It was a strong city-based team, made up of six players from the Emmets club, four from St Patrick's, two each from Celtic and Derry Guilds, and one from Emerald Harps, and they were optimistic of a breakthrough. They were granted home venue, and the match was fixed for 22 January 1922 but must have been brought forward by a week.

The War of Independence had ended with a truce the previous July, and the IRA was now the army of the new Free State, but the situation in the north was still fraught with tension. On Saturday 14 January 1922 six cars from Monaghan set out for the game but only got as far as Dromore before they were stopped, and ten members who were in the new Free State army were seized by the B Specials. The team included Dan Hogan, officer in command of the 5th Northern Division of the old IRA. He was the brother of Mike Hogan of Grangemockler, who had been shot dead while playing for Tipperary at Croke Park on Bloody Sunday eighteen months earlier (and commemorated today by the Hogan Stand). The others taken were T. Quigley, Edward O'Carroll, Joseph Brannigan, James McKenna, Thomas Mason, Patrick McGrory, James Murphy, James Winters, and Thomas Donnelly.

Details of the incident are still the subject of confidentiality restrictions. The team was travelling in six cars to Derry for the game. The Specials who surrounded the cars and seized them were later to claim that they found documents on them relating to plans to release three prisoners, Leonard, McShea, and Johnstone, due to be hanged in Derry jail. The Monaghan players were not charged and were well treated during their captivity, but twelve other political prisoners—Patrick Tully, Francis Gallagher, Patrick Maguire, Patrick O'Reilly, Francis Sheridan, James FitzPatrick, Bernard Sweeney, James McNulty, Patrick McAteer, High Timmins, Henry O'Loan, and Peter Donnelly—faced unspecified charges the day after the kidnapping.

Pro and anti-treaty factions, north and south of the border, united in efforts to get the players released. As

Derry city had decided to declare its allegiance to the Dáil rather than the new Belfast regime, things turned nasty. On 8 February, forty-two loyalists were kidnapped by the IRA and held as hostages for the footballers. It was a time of fear and of anger. A meeting of the North Derry Board in Claudy on 13 February was forced to disperse under a hail of bullets from the A Specials. The board had just been founded the previous October and was enjoying success in organising nine clubs under chairman W. Doherty and secretary John O'Kelly. The car in which the Dungiven delegates were travelling was stopped and its occupants beaten with rifle butts. Only for the arrival of an officer the delegates might have joined the dozens of Catholics who did not survive to sample life in post-treaty Ireland as the newly formed Specials, terrified that their own world was collapsing in around them, gave vent to their fear and anger.

Eventually the three prisoners were reprieved and the hostages released on 16 February, after the intervention of Michael Collins. Belfast was still unwilling to honour its side of the agreement reached between the sides, before instructions were eventually passed to Sir James Craig from Winston Churchill and the footballers released on 20 February.

None the worse for its experience as the first Free State football team to enjoy the hospitality of the Belfast administration, Monaghan lined out for the first round of the 1922 championship on 7 May. The match was postponed while the players spent those five weeks in jail, but in the confusion afterwards arranging a replay proved difficult, and Monaghan represented Ulster in the All-Ireland semi-final against Dublin in June.

Nearly twelve months passed before the final was eventually played. In the meantime Derry had been eliminated from the 1922 championships at the hands of Cavan, 4-4 to 1-1 at Cavan on 13 August 1922. The new border was causing more than a little discomfort for GAA followers that year, and most of the matches in the championship were held south of the border.

"The Ulster Council are nothing if not persistent," the Dublin newspaper *Sport* commented. Their persistence had to extend to finding their entire funds: the account had been transferred so often from bank to bank that the treasurer claimed he had mislaid them. Three provincial finals in all were played in 1923, four if you include the drawn 1922 final.

The delayed 1921 final was played in October. But Derry were seriously disheartened by events earlier that year. On 17 June 1923 they had defeated Donegal by 1-3 to 1-2 at Letterkenny, but on 12 August Cavan beat Donegal in the semi-final at Bundoran, indicating that Derry had been eliminated on objection. Derry put up very little fight in the 1921 replay, played on 28 October 1923, after the 1922 and 1923 finals had been completed, before a miserable gate of £7 15s (indicating an attendance of about 175).

Monaghan confirmed their nomination to represent Ulster as provincial champions that year when they won by 2-2 to 0-1. The *Freeman's Journal* reported: "Derry travelled to Clones on Sunday to meet Monaghan in the post final of 1921. It will be remembered that in the winter of that year the Monaghan selection started to travel to Derry to meet the latter in that year's final and on reaching Dromore in the Co. Tyrone the motors in which they travelled were surrounded by Specials and the entire team arrested and imprisoned for a considerable time. Sunday's match therefore saw the finish of the delayed fixture. In the absence of the official referee, Mr. Joseph McMahon, formerly of Cavan, held the whistle. The attendance was sparse and the sod was in a soaked condition. Derry had spent four and a half hours getting to Clones by motor which had a telling effect on the fitness of the team which no doubt played under difficulties."

At a meeting of the Ulster Council afterwards the secretary, P. McFadden, "read reports on the reorganisation of some of the Ulster counties, Donegal, Derry, Tyrone and Fermanagh which showed strong revival of Gaelic spirit hampered by many difficulties placed in the way of Gaelic football by the administration of the Belfast government."

The disqualification dealt the GAA in the county a grievous blow. Derry did not field in the 1924 or 1925 championships, and it was 1925 before Magherafelt priest P. J. Downey, Joe Mellon, Thomas O'Kane and Seán Mullan from Glenullin heralded a short-lived revival when they restarted Derry County Board. Seán Mullan attended the 1926 Ulster convention at Clones. A large crowd attended an exhibition game in Bellevue Park, Magherafelt, in April 1926. Father Downey's club, Magherafelt Pioneers, won the new county championship in 1926 when Glenullin, Kilrea, Lavey Erin's Own and Newbridge also took part, and on 3 April 1927 Ballinderry defeated Magherafelt Pioneers. The final of the 1927 championship between Glenullin and Ballinderry in October 1927 was abandoned after a riot, and after Gelnullin's disqualification Ballinderry defeated Drumsurn in the final.

Back in the Ulster senior championship in 1926, the Derry county team was beaten by Tyrone 3-3 to 2-1 on 6 June in Dungannon. In 1927 they succumbed to Cavan by 7-7 to 4-3 on 22 May in Belfast, and conceded seven goals again in 1928 as they perished at the hands of Tyrone 7-3 to 2-3 on 27 May in Dungannon. Derry played in the first Dr McKenna Cup match on 13 March 1927, losing to Antrim by 1-4 to 0-2 with a team that included some players from Carndonagh in Donegal.

Derry re-established their county board once more in 1929, with schoolteachers O'Brien and Wallace and Seán Ó Maoláin involved, and once more there were thirty-two counties in competition. Seán Ó Maoláin's brother Pat served as secretary for many years. They competed at junior level, defeating Antrim's second team in Derry by 1-5 to 0-4 but losing to Armagh's reserves by 3-14 to 0-2 in the Ulster final in Derry on 27 October. Despite initial promise, it was sixteen years before Derry escaped from the ignominy of junior status.

Ironically, it was in 1929 that Derry City were founded, reinforcing Derry city's allegiance to the non-handling code.

Magherafelt transferred to County Antrim for GAA purposes during this time, Newbridge St Trea's entered the south-west Antrim league, and Ballinderry played in

Tyrone for a time, although players remained eligible for selection for Derry. Burt had started playing in Derry as early as 1888, Portlough and Killea in 1889 and Newtowncunningham in 1890, Letterkenny in 1906, and Carndonagh in 1907; and in 1930 United Services, an army team, beat St Patrick's by 2-4 to 0-5 in the county final with reputed players from seven counties on the team. The following year Burt completed the hurling-football double. In July 1934 the Donegal clubs were instructed by the Ulster Council to revert to their own county, although some Derry city league competitions still involve Donegal clubs.

Derry needed help to make their sporadic appearances on the GAA records of those lean years. By limiting the 1930 McKenna Cup to four counties, the Ulster Council ensured that a victory over Tyrone sent Derry into the final, but it was Fermanagh, not Derry, who created history by gaining their first major trophy, winning 2-7 to 0-3 in Enniskillen on 10 August. They did not enter the McKenna Cup again until 1937, and were eliminated by Tyrone, 4-4 to 2-5, from the 1931 junior football championships.

Barney Fay asked Paddy Larkin to re-form the county board, and a meeting was held in St Joseph's School on 9 April 1933. Paddy Larkin was teaching in Draperstown, and soccer was played on the fair-green. There was no inter-county football, he recalls. A challenge match was arranged between Newbridge, then playing in South-West Antrim, and Ballinderry, then competing in East Tyrone. A large crowd watched the game in Ballinascreen. In 1933 Derry reached the Ulster junior football final. The team, largely made up of Ballinderry and Newbridge players such as Gerry Conway, Paddy Larkin, John and Mick McGuckin, Mickey McKenna, and Mickey Mullan, lost to Donegal by 3-7 to 1-3 at Letterkenny on the local CBS grounds. The pitch was not of the regulation size, but the result was allowed to stand. They were beaten in the final again two years later, this time by Armagh, 3-6 to 3-2 in Armagh. In 1933 Derry made their National League debut, losing to Tyrone 0-12 to 0-7 on 12 November 1933.

A separate Derry county convention had to be fixed for 1936 to sort out the lingering difficulties between the city and county boards. All the officials of the city board had resigned in July 1935, causing Derry not to fulfil their junior hurling championship fixture with Donegal (travel arrangements were used as an excuse to escape Ulster Council censure). A North Derry Board was started that year.

For a time in the 1930s Edward O'Brien served as Ulster delegate to the Central Council, while Michael Collins served as treasurer and president of the council. When Northern Ireland prime minister Basil Brooke asserted in 1946 that there was a difference between people in the Six and the Twenty-Six Counties, it was Collins who was to tell him: "We speak for a large percentage of the people of the nine counties of Ulster, and we want to tell him that neither height nor might, nor Brookes nor borders, will ever separate us."

It was, in retrospect, nothing short of a Derry renaissance that began in the National League of 1938. A competition that was to bring Derry a great helping of success had thirty entries that year, and divided them into one group of seven, one of six, and one of five, and Antrim in one of four groups of three counties.

Fittingly in a competition that was to be so kind to Derry, the team scored their first competitive victory over Antrim for eighteen years when a team that included Larry Brolly and Derry's first Railway Cup player, Paddy "Sticky" Maguire, came back from a point behind to beat Antrim by 3-5 to 1-9 in Belfast. They followed it up with a win over Tyrone by 1-8 to 1-7 two weeks later at Newbridge, and defeated Leitrim by 1-5 to 0-5 in a play-off at Newbridge the following 12 March.

In the quarter-final two weeks later the Derry county chairman personally guaranteed Roscommon £100 if they would travel to Derry. Gate receipts were £200 for the game, indicating a four thousand attendance, and the match was a great occasion, with a parade through Magherafelt and an escort from the border for a Roscommon team that was to win two successive All-Irelands within five years. Derry went out by a single point, 2-7 to 3-3.

Jim McKeever's first experience of an inter-county GAA match was that game between Derry and Leitrim and the following week's match against Roscommon. "I was very young. I went with my father. He knew Jimmy Murray, because his mother had come from Magherafelt. But they weren't famous at that stage. I thought football was big, but it was big in a local sense. The heroes at that stage were the local Newbridge team, Barney Murphy, John

McGrogan—fellows who were not known any more than fifty miles from home. To me they were heroes at that stage."

In the competition of the following year, 1939, Derry had only Tyrone in their section, and beat them by 1-5 to 0-6 in Omagh on 15 October and 5-5 to 3-5 in Newbridge a fortnight later to qualify for a play-off against Sligo for a quarter-final place. This time they conceded home advantage and were beaten by 1-9 to 0-2.

County secretary Seán Dolan was interned during the war, and died shortly after his release from prison on grounds of ill health in 1941.

Gaelic football struggled in Northern Ireland during the war years, and was allocated 100 footballs in 1942, 150 in 1943, just 20 in 1944 and 175 in 1945 by the Belfast Ministry of Supplies under war-time regulations. A match between St Columb's and Seán Dolans fixed for Derry city in 1943 was not played, as there was no ball. The smuggling of balls kept the game going in Derry and the border counties.

Despite the restrictions, the football revival that had started in 1938 was still in progress. Derry forced a draw with Antrim in the 1941 McKenna Cup when they had their youngest ever player, fifteen-year-old Paddy Douglas, on the team. Douglas was lost to the county at eighteen.

Also lost to Antrim was the star of the Derry war-time teams, Paddy "Sticky" Maguire, who was selected for the Ulster team at left-half-forward in 1943 and scored the winning goal as Ulster beat Leinster in what may have been the greatest Railway Cup final of all time. Lavey full-back

Jack Convery was selected for Ulster in 1945 before his nineteenth birthday.

In 1944 Convery, Thomas McCloskey, Mickey Lynch and Anthony Joe McGurk played with Derry in a great Lagan Cup campaign that saw them defeat Paddy "Sticky" Maguire's Antrim by 4-6 to 1-10, then Down and Armagh, to win their first major football trophy. This team was to win six more competitions in the coming years, scoring eleven goals in the 1944 Lagan Cup, seventeen goals in the 1945 junior championship, ten goals in the 1946/47 League, four against Fermanagh in the 1946 championship, and six against Armagh in Clones to win the Dr McKenna Cup.

Roddy Gribben had joined the side in 1945 when Derry won the Ulster junior championship for the first time, beating Antrim by 5-7 to 0-15, Donegal by 3-13 to 0-10, Tyrone by 5-3 to 1-6, and Armagh by 4-1 to 0-6 in a historic final at Belfast's Corrigan Park on 13 May. There was no All-Ireland junior championship at the time, but it encouraged Derry to re-enter the Ulster senior championship for the same year, and they put up a creditable show, going down by 3-7 to 2-3 against Donegal at Letterkenny on 10 June. Roddy Gribben remembers that travel restrictions were in force at the time, and the team got the service bus from Magherafelt to Derry, got another service bus from there to Letterkenny, stayed overnight in Letterkenny, and took a service bus home to Derry at eight o'clock that night.

The reintroduction of the hand-pass in 1946 gave a timely boost to Derry's GAA revival. First shock treatment was administered to the 1943 junior champions and 1945

SLOW STARTERS, 1884–1947   77

Ulster finalists, Fermanagh, who faced Derry in the 1946 championship. On 9 June at Magherafelt, Derry beat them by a whopping 4-6 to 0-4. Three weeks later Antrim ended their run with a close-run 1-11 to 0-10 win in the Ulster semi-final at Corrigan Park.

Derry took stock and waited for revenge. That year's winter Lagan Cup competition had been designated a division of the National Football League.

There is a neat explanation of how Derry won the 1946/47 National Football League title. It goes like this. The winter of 1947 was so bad that the GAA, rather than complete the League fixtures, invited the four divisional leaders to play in the semi-finals. That explains how Derry played Longford and Clare played Laois in the semi-finals. But the story is unfair to Derry, who in fact had completed their Lagan Cup programme at the time and had some notable victories under their belt.

Conditions were atrocious throughout, but Derry's consistency was unmistaken. On 20 October they defeated Armagh by 2-9 to 1-5 on a flooded field in Armagh. On 10 November they defeated Tyrone by 3-6 to 2-3. On 17 November they went to Ballybofey and in a downpour won by 1-7 to 1-4, finishing the match in semi-darkness. On 25 November, again on a waterlogged pitch in Magherafelt, they dropped their only point, drawing 2-5 to 2-5 with junior champions Down with goals from Francie Niblock and J. McElhone, with H. Brown scoring both of Down's goals.

The few hundred spectators present on 1 December

1946 at a muddy Magherafelt pitch could hardly have realised the significance of what they were about to see: the day that football in Derry turned the corner.

Antrim were the people's champions of 1946, an All-Ireland that was rightfully theirs bludgeoned from their hands by Kerry's use of the third-man tackle in the semi-final. Antrim too were undefeated in the Lagan Cup, and when they went down by 0-5 to 0-4 football followers everywhere took notice. It was widely circulated that the pitch was a factor and that Antrim's crack forwards had been bogged down in the mud. Pat Keenan remembers that it was flooded from top to bottom. "It made no difference when we started, but as the game went on it got worse. George Watters and Andy McCallin were great free-takers for Antrim, and in the last five minutes they couldn't lift the ball out of the mud." Antrim player John Gibson collapsed from the cold after the match.

When followers learnt that Derry should have won by more, and in fact had missed a penalty, their curiosity was further aroused. Derry had reason to be proud of their performance: Sonny McCann kept the Antrim hero, Kevin Armstrong, in check, and the frustrated Antrim selectors brought on Morgan at left-half-forward and moved Spence to midfield to try to counter Mick McNaught and Roddy Gribben. The scoring is easily summarised: McGillin for Antrim, McClone, John Eddie Mullan and Francie Niblock for Derry, Morgan and McAteer for Antrim, 0-3 each at half time, Mick McNaught and McElhone for Derry, Spence for Antrim, and a valiant rearguard action by Derry to secure victory. "It wasn't a kicking day," Keenan recalls. That was where Derry earned their National League laurels. There was no short-cut to the 1947 National Football League semi-final.

It is true that blizzard piled on blizzard across Ireland, and the Central Council was panicked into bringing the National League to a speedy conclusion. It is true that training was not exactly arduous: "up and down the field twice" is Pat Keenan's summary of it. In 1945 the Ulster Council had decided that the Lagan Cup should serve as the northern division of the National League, so on 30 March 1947 Derry defeated Longford by 2-11 to 2-2 in the National League semi-final.

There was no mistaking the tactics. The *Irish Independent* of 31 March reported tellingly: "The Antrim style of football is spreading. Its latest exponents, Derry, showed clearly that they had taken a few hints from the hand-passing and individual efforts displayed during the past few months by the Ulster championships when they defeated Longford in the National Football League semi-final at Derry yesterday. Indeed, this Derry team could be called a second Antrim. Their defence, built around Jack Convery, full back, and Sonny McCann, centre half, was sufficiently sound. Their centre field pair, Roddy Gribben and Mick McNaught, carried the superiority a step further. And their forwards did not give the Longford defence a moment's rest during the game. Led by centre half forward and Railway Cup player Francie Niblock, the whole six combined ideally, each player always running into position so there was always a man over to carry on a movement. It was this superiority in attack which proved the key to Derry's success. All through the first half it was a struggle between the Longford defence and the Derry forwards, and it was only poor finishing which forced the Ulster fifteen to be satisfied with a four points lead at the interval."

Derry beat Clare by 2-9 to 2-5 in the final, perhaps the first to be played on a Monday in Croke Park, on Easter weekend, 7 April 1947. Pat Keenan remembers staying in the long-departed Blessington Hotel for this match, half-frozen in a draughty room with few blankets. Most of the supporters at the match were from Derry, or for the colleges inter-provincial on the same afternoon. There were few Clare supporters in the ground when the match began.

Clare's crunching tackling took the Derry men by surprise. Francie Niblock had three teeth knocked out. Roddy Gribben was felled in the centre of the field. Pat Keenan used his speed to escape. Despite starting with a goal from Mullan, Derry trailed 1-4 to 1-5 at half time. They were a point behind again, 1-7 to 2-5, when Niblock scored what was one of the finest goals ever seen at Croke Park, a shot that he half-volleyed into the net off the upright from twenty yards. Larry Higgins and Pat Keenan, scoring his fifth point, finished the scoring. Francie Niblock scored 1-2 and Larry Higgins 1-1 of Derry's total.

"Derry won through the brilliance of their forwards," the *Irish Independent* reported. "The style compares favourably with the Antrim toe to hand and hand-passing methods. Here was another proof that no answer has been found to fast-moving forward play such as was adopted by Derry in the game. The answer given yesterday was to pull the man down, and as often as not it was not the player in possession who was fouled. The game itself was of a rugged nature, particularly when the Derry forwards were in possession. Pat Keenan, Francie Niblock and Larry Higgins displayed rare speed and combination in the half line and it was this trio which turned the game against Clare in the second half."

So Derry had their first national title, won without any Central Council assistance. Other counties long for such a breakthrough: Roscommon did not achieve it until 1979, Monaghan until 1985. Kildare have had five heartbreaking attempts. Yet Derry, two years after their return to senior ranks, had achieved it. Unfortunately there was no presentation ceremony, and the cup was sent to Derry the following Friday, enabling the celebrations to take place in Magherafelt. In a hilarious mock ceremony in Croke Park forty-five years later, GAA President Peter Quinn presented Pat Keenan with the cup that he should have received that Monday evening in Croke Park.

The seventeen-year-old Jim McKeever was under the Cusack Stand, having travelled on a bus from home. On his way to the match he remembers Roddy Gribben and John Murphy standing at a bus stop and his bus stopping to pick them up and bring them to Croke Park. He watched Tom Moriarty playing for Munster Colleges that day, little knowing he would be marking him in an All-Ireland semi-final a decade later.

The historic team included just one player from Derry city and another from north Derry, the rest from six clubs of the football parishes of the south: Charlie Moran (Glen), Séamus Keenan (Castledawson), Jack Convery (Lavey), Joe

Hurley (Lavey); John Murphy (Newbridge), Sonny McCann (Castledawson), T. E. McCluskey (Greenlough); Mickey McNaught (Seán Dolans, Derry), Roddy Gribben (Newbridge); Pat Keenan (Magherafelt), Francie Niblock (Magherafelt), Larry Higgins (Magherafelt); John Eddie Mullan (Dungiven), Paddy McErlean (Greenlough), John Cassidy (Greenlough)

4

DERRY ON CENTRE STAGE
1947–1958

The Oakboys had smelt success. Bellaghy full-forward
Hugh Glancy, a doctor and father of the current team
doctor, replaced Paddy McErlean in the team for the
McKenna Cup final, and on 25 May 1947 six thousand
people turned up in Clones to see Derry win the McKenna
Cup for the first time, totally dominating three-quarters of
their final against Armagh.

With twenty minutes to go Derry led by 6-1 to 0-2. Hugh
Glancy scored four of the goals according to the *Derry
Journal*, three according to the Dublin papers, T. E.
McCloskey a penalty and perhaps another goal, and
Francie Niblock a goal and a point. But when Armagh
moved veteran Jim McCullagh to centrefield, they started a
revival. Derry still won by a reasonably comfortable six-
point margin, 6-1 to 2-7.

After all that, Derry expected a good run in the
championship but were knocked out in Lurgan in the first
round by the only team to have drawn with them during
the winter, double junior champions Down, a team that
proved as adept at the flowing hand-passing movements as
Derry had been in the National League. Down frequently
took the ball the length of the field by this manner. Clancy
had a goal for Derry when they trailed by 1-5 to 0-1 and
reduced Down's half-time lead to 1-6 to 1-3; but when

McKibben scored a second goal for Down at the start of the second half, it was an uphill struggle for the Derry men. John Eddie Mullan scored the best goal of the game for Derry, and Down finished with a three-point rally, 2-11 to 2-5.

Down also defeated a promising 1947 Derry junior team, who beat Donegal by 4-3 to 1-1 and Tyrone by 1-4 to 0-5 before losing to Down in the final, 0-7 to 5-4, in Belfast.

Derry were defeated by Monaghan by three points in a torrential downpour in the 1948 championship. Pat Keenan, John Eddie Mullan and Roddy Gribben picked off 2-6 between them, but Derry never recovered from being seven points behind at half time. The following year they were heavily defeated by Antrim in the 1949 championship, 5-9 to 1-6 in Magherafelt. The pitch conditions of December 1946 were not replicated: Magherafelt field underwent radical development in the 1946–1950 period.

Just when Derry had evolved a style of football that was bringing them some success, congress abolished the hand-pass. Newspaper reporters at the first-round Ulster championship match at Corrigan Park, on 4 June 1950, in which Antrim beat Derry by 5-10 to 0-5, were quick to comment on how Antrim had not been affected by its removal. Considering Antrim had sponsored the abolition motion, that should not have caused many raised eyebrows.

The press failed to comment on how devastating the abolition of the hand-pass had been for Derry's game. Could it have been Derry's tactics at Magherafelt that the

Antrim men had in mind when they argued that the hand-pass should be done away with? The previous November, Derry had defeated Antrim by 5-6 to 1-5 in the Lagan Cup final. Pat Keenan scored three goals as Derry worked elaborate hand-passing movements through the Antrim defence. The local *Irish Independent* correspondent reported: "Not alone had Derry beaten Antrim as convincingly as the score suggests but they had won playing the type of football which the opposition has found so successful in recent years. Yet there was one significant, decisive difference. Derry had what Antrim sadly lacked, forwards who could finish off the hand-passing movements, not by trying to walk the ball into the goal but by scoring with forceful drives from twenty or thirty yards' range. These scores only served to emphasise one of the many weaknesses in the Antrim team which gave a thoroughly disappointing display. Derry's backs showed how this Antrim forward line could be held without conceding frees by the elementary method of each player marking his own man, and few gaps could be found at any stage.

That Dr Lagan Cup team was: C. Moran, S. Keenan, J. McGlone, J. Murphy, C. Hasson, M. McCann, O. Gribben, A. Lynch, M. McNaught, J. McKeever, J. Mullan, J. Hurley, Pat Keenan, M. Lynch, M. J. Cassidy. J. Hampson replaced Hasson.

That qualified Derry for the National League quarter-final and a meritorious performance against the reigning All-Ireland champions, Meath. Pat Keenan scored five points and McKeever three in that match, but Derry were leading when Meath had a lucky goal just before half time, the period that sports writers love to refer to as the psychological moment. A free from Frank Byrne was deflected to the goal by Mattie McDonnell, and Paddy O'Connell was in a position to score. Meath scored three points in the last four minutes to put an unkind blemish on the scoreline: a defeat that did not reflect Derry's true performance.

The *Irish Independent* described it as "a game which had many exciting moments and provided football which was well above the ordinary. Derry, the Dr Lagan Cup winners, fought valiantly from first to last and their clever hand-passing had Meath bewildered at times. On this display Derry will figure prominently in the forthcoming championships and with ordinary luck they will make a bold bid for the Ulster title."

It was not to be. Antrim again put paid to their championship ambitions. But morale remained high. Derry drew with Armagh in the McKenna Cup that year, and even after their championship defeat were invited out to Govan Park in Glasgow for a historic Gaelic football challenge on Saturday 18 June, losing this time by 3-11 to 2-8. But the result at Lurgan of a few weeks earlier, 21 May, was of great significance in the scheme of things to come.

Jim McKeever had opted to stay junior with Derry in 1950, and put in a stalwart performance before an injury affected his game as Derry beat Antrim by 2-7 to 1-4 to win the Ulster championship for the second time. C. McGurk and F. Niblock got the goals in a day on which Derry pride got a timely boost. Then they emulated the National League team of 1947 by reaching the All-Ireland final and a match against Mayo, the county's first in any grade of the championship. This was a far cry from the team humiliated by twenty points at Corrigan Park.

At Magherafelt on 24 June 1951, Derry surprised a fancied Monaghan team in the first round of the championship by 1-3 to 0-5. After twenty minutes of the first half a flying ball by C. Mulholland was flicked overhead into the goal by M. McCann. Derry led 1-1 to 0-2 at half time and were forced to withstand a fifteen-minute siege at the end, but the victory margin might have been greater had Mullan not hit the post in the second half. It was seen as an indication of success to come, as EDF reported in the *Irish Independent*: "From all viewpoints the game was thoroughly enjoyable and while the standard of play was never particularly high, a good crowd saw football fast, fierce and eager in well-nigh perfect conditions. Derry surprised even their most ardent supporters in withstanding Monaghan's hammer blows in the last quarter and could well prove a danger to the best in Ulster from now on. Without detracting a whit from the merits of Derry's victory, Monaghan were at a disadvantage on this undulating pitch. The raking wing to wing movements which are a feature of their play were entirely absent. Monaghan's defence was peculiarly susceptible to quick hand-passing and this mode of approach was successfully employed by Mullan, McCann and Roddy Gribben time after time, though they threw away scoring chances when the bastions were down."

A crowd of seven thousand turned up to see Derry lose to Cavan by a meritorious 1-6 to 1-4 in the Ulster semi-final in Davitt Park, Lurgan. A greasy ball hindered the game, but Derry were helped to settle by the fact that Cavan missed an early penalty and trailed by a respectable three points to two at half time. Then, five minutes into the second half, came the tragedy that cost Derry a break-through victory. Edwin Carolan sent in a harmless lob, goalkeeper C. Moran hesitated, and McEnroe sneaked in to pounce for a goal. When McEnroe pointed it was 1-4 to 0-2, and Derry never quite recovered, their frustration showing in inaccurate shooting. Moran made up for his early mistake with a great save from Carolan; this inspired the forwards, and Murphy scored for a hard left-footed drive. Mullan punched a point, and there was just one point in it. Cavan kept their cool, Pete Donohue pointed a free, and Derry's appearance in an Ulster final would have to wait.

Things were already going badly in Clones the following year when Derry trailed by 0-9 to 0-4 at half time. Then two Monaghan goals from Clarke and Brannigan inside two minutes of each other, ten minutes into the second half, put paid to Derry's championship hopes in 1952. The final score at Clones was 2-12 to 0-12, and Mick "Mackey" Moyna contributed five points to Monaghan's total.

Down's mini-revival of the 1940s had faded, and they were easily defeated in the first round of the championship by 1-11 to 2-5 at Magherafelt in May 1953. But in the Ulster semi-final against Armagh in the newly opened Casement Park in Andersonstown, Belfast, a relatively unknown Armagh forward named Art O'Hagan ran the Derry defence ragged. He had the ball in the net after just three minutes, and although Young gave Derry some encouragement when he fisted the equaliser, O'Hagan had the ball in the net twice more before half time. At the break it was 3-1 to 1-1, at the final whistle it was 4-11 to 1-5, and it was scarce consolation to Derry that Armagh went on to almost beat Kerry in an emotional All-Ireland final where fans broke down the gates to gain admission and Bill McCorry missed a famous penalty that could have changed the course of GAA history.

Derry's revenge over Armagh came in the McKenna Cup of the following spring, as they re-emerged to win the trophy for the second time with a series of late, late finishes. Such success looked a long way away when Jim McKeever was outplayed by Fermanagh's Joe Lennon at Irvinestown, and Derry trailed by three points at the end of normal time in the quarter-final. Then came goals from McKeever and Long Tom Doherty to metamorphose the match, and Derry won by 2-5 to 1-5.

Derry opened their new Dean McGlinchey Park in Ballinascreen before the McKenna Cup semi-final against Cavan. Dublin Crokes and UCD played in a hurling challenge the same day. W. Cassidy's late goal brought them back into the match and a place in the semi-final a fortnight later. Then, in beating Armagh by 1-8 to 2-4 in the final on 23 May, Derry trailed by seven points early in the second half before two scores from the Gribbens, Mick scoring the equaliser and Tommy the winner, brought them a 1-8 to 2-4 victory.

That McKenna Cup winning team was: M. McCann, R. McNicholl, E. Kealey, P. Kealey, M. Gribben, H. Cassidy, F. Stinson, P. Breen, J. McKeever, T. Gribben, T. L. Doherty, Roddy Gribben, C. Higgins, F. Devlin, C. Mulholland.

Derry heavily defeated Down in the 1954 championship at Newcastle, 4-11 to 3-4, before running into the defending Ulster champions at Casement Park. This time there was no late finish or McKenna Cup heroics. Armagh led by 0-10 to 0-1, and the late goal by Jim McKeever only served to put some respectability on the scoreline as Derry went out by 1-12 to 1-6. The *Irish Independent* reported: "To be charitable about it, it became more and more obvious as the game progressed that Derry were going through one of those days when nothing would go right. Their forward line became completely disjointed and it must have been heart-breaking for their solid defence to see their own first-half work going to naught at the other end of the field."

The 4,500 fans who gathered in Jim McKeever's home parish of Magherafelt to watch Derry play Tyrone in the first round of the 1955 Ulster championship did not suspect that they were watching the two coming teams of the Ulster championship. Derry won by 0-13 to 1-5, and set the scene up for a third tilt at Armagh.

The Ulster semi-final against Armagh at Casement Park on 3 July was as significant as any in Derry football history. Derry destroyed the hopes of the previous year's Ulster finalists by 3-4 to 0-2. Armagh were just a shadow of the team that had so narrowly failed to Meath, 1-9 to 1-8, in the National League semi-final the previous April. A goal from Roddy Niblock in the first half started the rout, "Chuck" Higgins scored a penalty six minutes from the end, and Colm Mulholland administered the coup de grâce two minutes later to put Derry into their first Ulster final since 1921.

Their opponents, Cavan, had beaten Derry by 3-6 to 0-9 in the McKenna Cup final, but Derry were confident that seven changes in their line-out would help rectify the situation, including the dropping of goalkeeper Paddy Gormley, later a hero of their All-Ireland appearance. Hugh Francis Gribben was the only change since the historic semi-final win over Armagh.

But Cavan had played in more Ulster finals than Derry had senior clubs, and the crowd of 24,800 who came to Clones knew what to expect. Although Cavan won by 0-11 to 0-8, it was a closer thing than most Derry men expected. Cavan goalkeeper Séamus Morris brilliantly saved a penalty from Charlie "Chuck" Higgins when Derry were trailing by 0-4 to 0-2 with just two minutes remaining in the first half. Roddy Gribben had the famed Phil "Gunner" Brady in his pocket for quite a spell in the first half. But unfortunately, Jim McKeever had a quiet first half and Cavan's Pete Donohue chose this match to come out of a three-year retirement and score eight points out of his side's total of eleven, contributing to two of the other three. He had been a substitute on the 1952 Cavan team and was out of football since. Roddy Gribben and Jim McKeever scored three points each of Derry's total, M. Gribben and F. Niblock the other two points.

The Ulster final team, Derry's first since the three-year delay had scuppered the chances of the Oakboys of 1920, was: J. Murphy; H. F. Gribben, E. Kealy, T. Doherty; M. Gribben 0-1, H. Cassidy, F. Stinson; P. Breen, Jim McKeever 0-3; F. Niblock 0-1, T. J. Doherty, E. Fullen; Charlie Chuck Higgins, Roddy Gribben 0-3, C. Mulholland; substitute O. Gribben for F. Stinson.

Despite the rapid decline of hurling in the county, Derry's camogie record remained strong, and in 1954 the county contested its first All-Ireland final. As early as 1934, Derry had ten camogie clubs in action. The 1954 team drew with Antrim in the Maguire Cup, and built on that progress to score a first Ulster final victory over Antrim and reach the All-Ireland final.

Their progress to the final was impressive: beating Down by 5-1 to 1-2, Antrim by 5-2 to 2-2, Mayo by 5-2 to nil, and London by 3-11 to 0-3. But in the final they faced a Dublin team whose dominance was unprecedented in any sport: they had not been beaten in competition since 1947, and names such as Kathleen Mills, Sophie Brack, Eileen Duffy and Eileen Bourke already stood out in the annals of the game while each was building up impossible totals of All-Ireland medals.

It was a remarkably clean game, yielding only one free in the fifty minutes of play. The result, 10-4 to 4-2, was a fair reflection of Dublin's dominance. Derry managed to launch a series of early attacks without reward, and Dublin opened with three goals before Derry settled down and had a half-time lead of 6-2 to 0-1, P. O'Brien having scored Derry's points. Derry's second-half goals came from R. McAllister, Patsy McCloskey, Pat O'Brien, and A. Bryson, and a point from Patsy McCloskey got a good reaction from the crowd. Theresa Halferty, Carrie Rankin, Patsy McCloskey and Pat O'Brien were all later to win places on the Ulster team for the inaugural Gael-Linn inter-provincial series, but Derry's senior camogie final appearance was of little benefit to the game in the county.

A. McPeake (Lavey), T. Clarke (Greenlough), Theresa Halferty (Lisnamuck), Carrie Rankin (Greenlough), M. Dorrity (Lavey), M. McSwiggan (Lisnamuck), Patsy McCloskey (Greenlough), K. McCloskey (Greenlough), K. Madden (Greenlough), Pat O'Brien (Lisnamuck), A. Bryson (Lisnamuck), R. McAllister (Greenlough). Substitutes: A. Cassidy (Greenlough), P. McPeake (Lavey), K. Connor.

The 1978 junior championship winning team was: Patricia McCloskey (Glenullin), May Lee (Bellaghy), Brigid McLaughlin (Glack), Sarah Ann Quinn (Swatragh), Eileen McQuillan (Swatragh), Margaret Convery (Glen), Bríd McWilliams (Swatragh), Sharon Loftus (Kilrea), Kathleen Marrion (Greenlough), Caroline McWilliams (Swatragh), Brigid McCloskey (Greenlough), Bernadette Deighan (Ballerin). Substitutes: Bernadette McGowan (Drumsurn), Sinéad Burke (Drumsurn), Martina O'Kane (Swatragh), Cathleen McErlean (Greenlough). Kathleen O'Hagan, captain of the 1969 winning team, trained the 1978 team.

The winning habit in the junior championship was by now well established, as Derry took the title for the fourth time in a ten-year period on 15 May 1955 in Lurgan. They beat Down by 0-13 to 0-6, and once more went as far as an unsuccessful All-Ireland final. A crowd of 5,384 saw that 1955 junior team eventually meet their match in Navan when they faced Cork in the All-Ireland junior home final, going down by 3-10 to 1-7.

The team contained names that were shortly to become familiar throughout the country: P. Gormley, M. Donnell, W. Gribben, D. Cassidy, M. Higgins, G. Muldoon, P. Smyth,

S. Young, T. Stevenson, G. McCann, B. Murray, J. Fullen,
P. Heron, J. E. Mullan, F. Shiels. Substitutes: B. Mullan for
Higgins, M. O'Neill for Fullen, Higgins for Donnelly.

After Tyrone beat Derry by 3-7 to 2-4 in the driving rain at
Dungannon in the first round of the 1956 championship,
they went on to become the first "new" county to win an
Ulster title since 1900. Few suspected that this was about to
happen three times in four years, and Derry were to be the
second breakthrough team.

In Dungannon, Derry's first-half performance was
abysmal, both their points coming from fourteen-yard frees
as they trailed by two points 0-4 to 0-2 for Tyrone at half
time, and two points to 3-7 before they began a rattling
comeback. L. Regan scored two goals and Owen Gribben
and J. E Mullan the points. Two of Tyrone's goals were
scored by Dónal Donnelly, the third by Jim Conlan.

Derry showed they were serious about their Ulster
ambitions when they brought Kerry man Paul Russell to
train the 1957 team. Thirty years earlier Russell had been
one of the most sought-after players in the country,
winning All-Ireland medals with Kerry and Dublin and
once being selected by both Munster and Leinster for the
same Railway Cup competition. Now he trained Derry on
the principles established by Éamonn O'Sullivan for GAA
fitness.

The memory of many humiliations at the hands of
Antrim were exorcised on 9 June 1957, when Derry defeated
Antrim by eighteen points, 4-14 to 0-8, at Ballinascreen.
More old scores were settled in the rain at Dungannon when

Derry avenged their 1955 Ulster final defeat when they beat Cavan by a single point, 1-10 to 1-9. Jim McKeever was placed at centre-half-back to bolster Derry's defence in this watershed game. With the emigration of John Murphy, Tommy Joe Doherty was a late substitution to play in goal for Derry, and when he was called out to take a free after nine minutes, few suspected that disaster was in hand. Doherty's kick fell short, and Mick Lynch fly-kicked it straight back into the Derry net. But the match turned on an incident six minutes into the second half when a pass from the Cavan half-back line fell short, and Roddy Gribben swooped for a goal. Play was delayed by a prolonged search for the ball, which had disappeared into a clump of bushes, and it was clear that there would be a generous allowance for lost time when Derry took the lead for the first time, Larry Regan scoring a point just on the pip of time. Séamus Conaty levelled for Cavan with a point that might have been a goal, and the game stretched on and on until Seán O'Connell, a youthful student teacher playing in only his second match for Derry, totally unruffled by the tension, slotted over a calm winning point.

People in the county were talking of an Ulster success, several newspaper tipped Derry to beat Tyrone in the first final between two of the Six Counties since partition, and 36,500 fans converged on Clones for an Ulster final that would have been unthinkable five years before. Derry were mindful of the fact that they had lost to Tyrone in the 1956 championship and that in the previous winter's Lagan Cup final, after a draw in Lurgan, Tyrone won by 3-6 to 0-9 in Casement Park. They did have goalkeeper Paddy Gormley back and Willie Cassidy on for Larry Regan. Their optimism was confirmed when two frees from Seán O'Connell and a point from play gave Derry an early 0-3 to 0-2 lead. Then Frank Higgins finished a movement involving Patsy Devlin and Dónal Donnelly to the net mid-way through the first half. Derry were forced to fight their way back from five points down, trailed by 1-4 to 0-4 at half time, but levelled after seventeen minutes of the second half. Three frees from the outstanding young Seán O'Connell and a point from Pat Breen at long last led to the equaliser from S. Young. O'Connell scored eight points in all, seven from frees, equalling Pete Donohue's 1955 record for an Ulster final. In the last thirteen minutes it was Tyrone who rose to the challenge, Teggart and Frank Donnelly scoring before Seán O'Connell's final free three minutes from the end: Tyrone 1-9, Derry 0-10. Another might-have-been.

The Ulster final team was: P. Gormley; P. McLarnon, H. F. Gribben, T. Doherty; G. Muldoon, J. McKeever, P. Smith; P. Breen, O. Gribben; Seán O'Connell, Roddy Gribben, E. Fullen; W. Cassidy, T. Doherty, S. Young. Substitutes: S. O'Connor for Muldoon; C. Higgins for Cassidy; Muldoon for Gormley.

John Murphy's emigration was a symptom of the times. As Britain enjoyed a construction and industrial boom, up to fifty thousand Irish people were heading east each year. In 1958 the London GAA decided to take advantage of this rise in emigration and stage its most ambitious promotion to date and inadvertently helped Derry to break the psychological big-time barrier.

In the spring of 1958 Derry faced Tyrone in the semi-final of the new Wembley tournament, but as far as Derry were concerned there was much more than a trip to London's most famous sports stadium, venue for the Olympics of a decade earlier, at stake. Tyrone had been unbeaten in two years, and when Derry set about destroying that record they did so comprehensively. Derry led by seven points at half time and went on to win by 1-12 to 1-2 before an enthusiastic crowd at Ballinascreen. The *Irish Independent* reported: "Right from the start this uproarious Ballinascreen crowd sensed that a turn-up was in the air. With the wind behind them Derry streaked into a seven-point interval lead with Jim McKeever and Phil Stuart lording it over Jody O'Neill and Patsy Devlin at midfield, complete masters of all they surveyed, and Peter Smith at left-half and Tommy Doherty immediately behind him playing their hearts out. Derry were firing on all cylinders. They were a tough and strong goal-defending and point-snatching side, without any trimmings. Tyrone apparently had never heard of a youngster named Leo O'Neill, a first-year student at Queen's University. They know now; their defenders in the first quarter gave him the freedom of the pitch, and how they paid the penalty."

What matter that Galway won the Wembley honours before a 33,240 attendance? Despite the benefit of a first-minute lead with the help of a GAA rarity, an own goal, and Derry's midfield of Jim McKeever and Phil Stuart failing to live up to their potential as Frank Evers had a great game from Galway, Derry were now more comfortable with their status as a serious contender in the football world.

Against Donegal and Antrim that status was again not exactly apparent to the tiny groups of spectators who turned out to watch. "Seldom has such a dull and featureless championship match been seen," the *Irish Independent* reported after a 0-8 to 0-5 victory over Antrim, "for there was scarcely a ripple of excitement and certainly not a constructive movement during the hour. Except for a short spell early in the second half when Antrim, trailing five points in arrears, fought back to equality, there was nothing to cheer the small number of spectators present. On this form, Derry's reputation as one of the top teams in the province is surely undeserved, for they did not even look a good club team and it was also made abundantly clear that when circumstances forced them on the defensive their team work is liable to go to pieces. Yesterday the beautifully devastating link up between the midfielders and the defence and the attack which has stood them in such good stead was never evident. Only in patches did we notice the precision and perfect approaches of Jim McKeever who was only a pale shadow of his usual self. And the fact that he seemed off-form affected the rest of the team. Derry wasted many opportunities in the first half and with monotonous regularity their forwards were repeatedly wide of the mark. In this respect Dinny McKeever was a regular offender for time and time again he showed a clean pair of heels to the Antrim defence but his shooting was hopelessly wide of the mark."

But against Cavan in the Ulster semi-final, Jim McKeever showed that when he hit form, nothing could compete with him. As well as their regular midfield, Hugh

O'Donoghue and Jim McDonnell, Cavan switched four others—Tom Maguire, Séamus Conaty, Hubert Gaffney, and substitute Mick Shields—in to counter McKeever. Cavan, who had been five points up after fifteen minutes, ran into serious problems. Down at their muddy goal-mouth, goalkeeper and future award-winning playwright Tom McIntyre was picking the ball out of the Cavan net no fewer than four times ("'Twas the goalkeeper that beat ye," an unrecognising fan sympathised with McIntyre after-wards) as Derry ran into a 4-7 to 1-5 lead. Two Cavan goals in the last five minutes put a blemish on the scoreline, 4-7 to 3-6, and an Ulster final for Derry against fellow-newcomers to the big time, Down, the first Ulster final since 1890 in which neither team had previously won the Ulster championship.

Thoughts turned to the Lagan Cup semi-final of the previous November, when Down had delighted one of the largest crowds ever in Newcastle with a 1-13 to 3-3 victory. McKeever played the best football of the hour as Derry came back to within two points early in the second half, but there was no living with this autumnal Down, with Kevin Mussen in superb form.

Derry needed to match them in fitness and youth. With their age ranging from 20-year-old Leo O'Neill to 29-year-old Owen Gribben, youth was not a problem. Roddy Gribben and physical education instructor McKeever, one of the first PE GAA players in the country, took over the training and the evening sessions in Newbridge (in the rain, always in the rain that summer, forty days after St Swithin's Day without a yield, as farmers despaired and footballers sighed), and cemented a team spirit that had been latent before.

Oddly enough, the rain let up for that Ulster final, keeping the attendance down to 22,000. At half time Derry led by seven points to three, points from Jim McKeever, Denis McKeever, Seán O'Connell twice, Chuck Higgins twice, and Owen Gribben giving them the lead they needed. It was never going to be a classic Ulster final, whatever exactly a classic Ulster final is supposed to be, but when Chuck Higgins added a goal at the start of the second half, it was unlikely that the inexperienced Down team would recover. They did their best, getting goals back from Jim McCartan and a penalty goal from Paddy Doherty, stopped by goalkeeper Patsy Gormley but at the wrong side of the line, according to the umpire. Points from Leo O'Neill, O'Connell, Jim McKeever and Owen Gribben ensured that Derry eventually became champions by 1-11 to 2-4. John D. Hickey reported: "On the whole this was a disappointing affair and it lacked the essential atmosphere that makes a game, as distinct from the reward it brings a truly memorable test. Derry always seemed to have the title securely in their grasp. Their superior generalship throughout the field was never more strikingly illustrated than in the closing stages when Down cut their lead to three points. Apparently feeling in some danger the Derrymen retaliated by producing their best football of the hour and scored two points which caused Down supporters to abandon hope, as was demonstrated by their silence, following a crescendo of cheering."

It lashed heaviest of all for the All-Ireland semi-final, keeping the attendance down to a mesmerised 30,723 spectators in Croke Park, who watched Derry astound Kerry by 2-6 to 2-5 in the All-Ireland semi-final. The rain was so heavy that the pre-match parade was dispensed with, the De La Salle Brothers' Brass and Reed Band from Belfast striking up the national anthem and GAA president J. J. Stuart throwing in the ball. The story of the game is told by the wides rather than the scores—17 for Kerry and just 4 for Derry—but there was no doubting the hero of the hour: just when Derry were under intense pressure to hang on to a one-point lead, Seán O'Connell grasped a Peter Smith free and rattled in the winning goal three minutes from the end. Kerry panicked, Patsy Gormley in the Derry goal was called upon to make several heroic saves, and when Mick O'Connell landed a fifty into the goalmouth Tadhgie Lyne eventually scored a Kerry goal with a minute to go. Derry held out, and Kerry were left ruefully wondering what would have happened if they had taken points rather than rushed the goal in those desperate final minutes.

There were names other than O'Connell on the supporters' lips that day. Patsy McLarnon was selected as some commentator's man of the match. Jim McKeever hit a purple patch in the ten minutes before half time before Mick O'Connell was switched in to face him and he was disabled by a rattling collision with opponent John Dowling in the second half.

Yet it was Kerry who had got the early boost. Patsy Gormley thought that an angled Tadhgie Lyne free was going wide and let it roll painfully into the net. McKeever and Seán O'Connell set to, and there were just two minutes to go in the first half when Jim McKeever's ball dropped short, and his younger brother Denis scrambled it into the net in the melee. It meant that Derry had a two-point lead, 1-4 to 1-2, to show for thirty minutes of play with the wind, and when Roche was hauled down with the goal at his mercy, it looked as if Derry's championship was as good as over. For most of the second half Derry came under pressure as Paud Sheehan and Garret McMahon picked off three points in twelve minutes.

Derry treated the victory as their All-Ireland. A match-winning function took place in the Royal Hibernian Hotel afterwards, and the heroes were feted all the way home. "If we had really concentrated from the start of the season on the idea of winning the All-Ireland, it might have been different," McKeever reflected some years later.

It was back into training after that for the All-Ireland, but training was light by comparative standards. "I am a farmer, and we were trying to get the corn in while the All-Ireland was coming on. I can remember Éamonn Young coming up from Cork to write about the game, and when he came we had to cut the corn with scythes and it was real hard work. It was a rush to get it in."

Win, lose, or draw, it was inconceivable to Derry followers that such a young team would take twelve years to get out of Ulster again, and that only Seán O'Connell would survive to play in an All-Ireland semi-final again.

This Derry team were as much children of the 1948 Northern Ireland Education Act as children of the wetlands of the Sperrins or Loughshore, the traditional nurseries of

Derry Gaelic football. It carried names already familiar to Derry football followers—Gribben, Mullan, McKeever—and drew heavily on traditional GAA strongholds: Newbridge, Ballerin. But these players came from a wide and exotic variety of backgrounds, elementary and grammar school, the four farmers being matched now by four teachers (two of them in physical education), with the cattle dealer, bricklayer, labourer and fitter being supplemented by a chemist's assistant, a medical student, and an art student. Many were veterans of top-level college competition. St Patrick's in Armagh had provided three of the players, St Malachy's and St Columb's two each. Three of them had played in Croke Park for St Mary's training college. Six of them had played on Derry's 1953 Ulster junior championship winning team. With an average age of twenty-four years and eight months, average height of 5 feet 10, and average weight slightly over 12 stone, the team was regarded as young and rather small by the standards of the time.

Patsy Gormley from Claudy, a 24-year old cattle dealer, stood 5 feet 10 and weighed 11 stone. Renowned for his strong, safe hands in goal, he had learnt his football with local public elementary school, played senior club football for Foreglen at fourteen, played midfield with Derry minors in 1952, moved to goalkeeper for the junior team, winning an Ulster medal in 1953, and had been in and out of the senior team since, holding the regular spot after Derry's usual goalkeeper, John Murphy, emigrated in 1956. He played well despite being involved in a car accident the night before the game, but did not play after 1960.

Patsy McLarnon from Newbridge was just twenty-three at the time of the All-Ireland, stood 5 feet 10 and weighed 12 stone 7. He had learnt his football at Castledawson school, worked his way through minor and junior to senior with the Newbridge club, and helped them with the 1955 club championship. When he was selected for the county minor side in 1952 it was at centre-back, moved to left-corner for county junior side in 1953, and went to right-corner for the All-Ireland final. His reputation was as a tenacious defender with a great turn of speed, good judgement, a good sense of positional play, clean handling skills, and strong tackling. He played on until 1961, and is a building contractor now in Magherafelt.

Hugh Francis Gribben, a 22-year-old farmer, stood 5 feet 11 and weighed 12 stone 4. One of six footballing brothers, he learnt his football at Anahorrish school, and graduated to the Newbridge club side, which was synonymous for years with the Gribben family. He has played midfield, half-back and full-back with distinction. He was also heavily involved in Newbridge's pitch development. A member of the 1955 Ulster junior team, his excellent fielding, cool anticipation and lengthy clearances earned him a place on the senior team. He played on until 1968, and now farms in County Meath.

The Gribbens' father was a supporter and contributor to the GAA, and sent the boys to watch All-Ireland finals in Dublin as their annual holiday: bus to Belfast, train to Dublin; gone on Friday and back on Tuesday. Willie Gribben played minor; Owen was centre-half-back for years, finishing at full-forward in 1958; Michael was injured in the 1958 Ulster final and never played inter-county again; Hugh Francis played full-back in 1958; Henry went to Edinburgh to become a vet.

Tommy Doherty from Lavey, a 28-year-old, 5 feet 9, 12 stone 7 bricklayer, had earned the nickname "Wee Tommy Doherty" to distinguish him from his towering cousin of the same name who was known as "Long Tommy" when he joined the Derry team in 1954. He played with Colm Mulholland at Ballymacpeake school and worked his way through minor and junior ranks to the Derry senior team. He played left-back for the Derry minors in 1949, centre-half-back and left-back for Lavey, and was left-back on that fateful day when he slipped and left Paddy Farnan with a clear run at the Derry goalmouth for the winning goal. His son Damien went on to win an All-Ireland club medal with Lavey in 1991, while Peter is a noted hurler.

Patsy Breen, a teacher from Desertmartin, was twenty-five, stood 5 feet 10 and weighed 12 stone. He had won three Ranafast Cup medals with St Patrick's College, Armagh, represented Ulster at colleges level, was a star in Desertmartin's comprehensive demolition of Ballerin in the 1953 county championship final, and had filled no fewer than eight positions on the field. He started off as Jim McKeever's ideal midfield partner, and ended up with a reputation as one of the outstanding right half backs in the country. Patsy went on to become principal of Moneymore primary school, played on until 1960, and later coached a number of teams.

Colm Mulholland, a farmer from Lavey, was twenty-eight, stood 6 feet tall, and weighed 12 stone 7. He had

captained the Derry minor team in 1948, was promoted to
junior and senior in quick succession, and then moved
back to junior to win an Ulster championship in 1950 as a
midfielder. A left-half-forward on the senior side so heavily
beaten by Armagh in the 1953 Ulster semi-final, he moved
to left-corner-forward on the team that won revenge
against Armagh in the 1954 McKenna Cup final. A family
bereavement and a broken leg cost him his place on 1956
and 1957 teams, but his majestic fielding, strong tackling
and powerful kicking with Lavey won his place back on the
county team. His cousin Éamonn Diamond played for the
county before moving to England, his brother Brian also
played for Lavey, and his son Don now plays with the club.

Medical student Peter Smith played with Littlebridge
before they became defunct and joined from Ballinderry.
He was twenty-four at the time of the All-Ireland, stood 5
feet 7 and weighted 12 stone. He had won a Ranafast Cup
medal in 1951 with St Patrick's College in Armagh, was
selected at minor in 1952 and for the 1953 junior
championship team, and used to play as a forward before
making a name as a wing-half-back, a tremendous kicker of
a dead ball, a distributor of long, judicious clearances, and
a sure and keen tackler with a penchant for turning defence
into attack. Scorer of a point in the final, within four years
he was lost to the county team and is now a gynaecologist
in Libya, where he works as an external examiner to
medical students.

At that time twenty-seven years old, Jim McKeever from
Ballymaguigan captained the team, stood 5 feet 10 and
weighed 11 stone 6. He was already regarded as one of the

greatest midfielders of all time, had spent eight seasons on the Ulster team, and been selected to play for All-Ireland teams in representative games. He also played basketball for Ulster. The modest, shy, quietly spoken Jim provided the groundwork for much of Derry's success. He started playing with Ballymaguigan school, then St Malachy's, and was chosen for the 1948 county minor team, and the county senior team at seventeen years of age. As a youngster he admired Mick Higgins of Cavan. An Antrim minor in 1947, a Derry minor in 1948, and a Derry senior 1948–1962, in 1950 he flew back from England to play a significant part in Derry's Lagan Cup success and was behind every Derry breakthrough of the 1950s afterwards, becoming an Ulster senior medallist in 1958, twice beaten in Ulster and National League finals, two Railway Cup medals with Ulster, footballer of the year in 1958, junior Ulster medallist in 1950, manager of Ulster's Railway Cup successes in 1970 and 1987, and three times a county championship medallist. He went on to become a lecturer at St Mary's Training College, training the college team for thirty-five years, including its surprise Sigerson Cup success, and is now retired and living in Belfast with his wife, Theresa. They have three daughters, Ann, Maeve, and Deirdre, and two sons, Éamonn and Jim. During his career he played for Newbridge and Ballymaguigan in Derry, Leicester Young Irelands in England, and Downpatrick in Down. In 1993 he trained the Derry under-21 hurlers to the Ulster championship. He doesn't think the game has changed as much as people say. "Players are now fitter. There is more support play. While there is more sophistication in management and preparation, the general standard has come up because of that. The team had been making progress and had come close to beating Cavan in 1955, so it wasn't that surprising to win the Ulster final. What was surprising was beating Kerry in the All-Ireland semi-final, that was simply incredible. We gradually accumulated experience and more confidence. The team had not changed that much in personnel in three or four years. A lot of positional changes had taken place but we had grown in confidence, we had learnt a lot about football, and also when you get to a final for the third time it is time to win it.

"One of the thoughts all of us had was that we will be back. It was a young team. We ought to have been back but we didn't. I am sure it would have been easier the second time round: the winning becomes more important. To come back is important.

"When I grew up the catch was the feature which people tended to focus on, particularly at club level; at home to get possession was the prize. The way to win the ball was to catch, and I learnt at an early age that to catch it was important, and if you get reasonably proficient at it it is a big advantage. I can't remember deliberately practising it. I was a boarder in St Malachy's College, and boarders spent a lot of time kicking football, and we used to do a lot of kicking into goals; there were so many people there that you could spend a long time and not get a kick unless you won the ball, so it really was a competition every afternoon to see how many kicks you could get inside twenty minutes or fifty minutes or whatever. When I began to have some success in getting more kicks than everybody else it reinforced the need for catching the ball. We trained ourselves to catch the ball just for the sake of getting possession."

His midfield partner was a student, Phil Stuart, a 21-year-old who stood 5 feet 11 and weighed in at 12 stone 5, now lecturer in Irish at St Mary's College in Belfast. First noticed by Derry minor selectors in 1954, he played in the 1956 junior county side and partnered Patsy Breen in midfield for the Lagan Cup campaign. His fielding and determination took much of the work off Jim McKeever's shoulders that summer, and he went on to play with Derry until 1967 and later coached Queen's Sigerson Cup teams.

Seán O'Connell, already nicknamed "the Big Fellow" or "the General," was to outlast all his team-mates. He made his club debut with Ballerin in 1953. By the time of the All-Ireland final he was twenty-one, weighed 13 stone and stood 6 feet 2, and had earned a reputation as a stylist, able to score from long range. Tall and rangey, he uses height and weight to excellent advantage and carries a deceptive body swerve. He learnt his football in St Columb's before going on to St Mary's Training College, and in 1956 partnered Denis McKeever on the St Mary's team that defeated their Dublin counterpart, St Patrick's, Drumcondra, by nine points to one, a week after St Patrick's club team, Erin's Hope, had won the Dublin senior championship. Scorer of four points in the final, he played on until 1976, winning four Ulster medals, four Railway Cup medals, and training Derry teams that won All-Ireland minor and under-21 titles in 1965 and 1968. (When a contestant in a north Derry Scór quiz was asked who in

Irish history was known as the Big Fellow, he protested when they would not award him the points for "Seán O'Connell.")

Brendan Murray, a chemist's assistant from Ballerin, later to become a pharmacist in Ballymena, was twenty-four, stood 5 feet 11, and weighed 11 stone 4. The nephew of Tyrone 1940s player Leo Daly, he played McRory Cup for St Malachy's, was a minor in 1952, and made the Derry senior team after an injury to clubmate Brian Mullan. Centre-half-back with his club, he missed Ballerin's 1957 county championship success over Ballymaguigan because he was playing with St Gall's in Belfast. He won a reputation as a cool and brainy player who figured in all the forward positions, having had a run at midfield while in college and whose clever, methodical distribution of the ball led to many scores. He played on at corner-back until 1963.

A 23-year-old physical education teacher, Denny McKeever from Ballymaguigan stood 5 feet 10 and weighed 11 stone and had rapidly emerged from the shadow of brother Jim, scoring a goal off Seán Murphy in the All-Ireland semi-final. He started in St Trea's school in Ballymaguigan, played minor, junior and senior with Newbridge, winning a county championship medal in 1955 before declaring for Ballymaguigan, and played county junior in 1953 and 1955. While playing with St Mary's Training College in Belfast, he was selected for the Derry team. He was showing great powers of acceleration and a tendency to wander far afield in search of the ball, and an ability to cut a straight path to goal when in possession. He scored a point in the All-Ireland final, played on until 1961, and was a selector on the 1993 team that won the All-Ireland.

Brian Mullan from Ballerin, a 23-year-old farmer who stood 5 feet 10 and weighed 12 stone, came from a famous Derry football family; his brothers Michael and Patsy played for the county team. Brian played full-back for St Columb's and then moved to attack, where his reputation for speed and accurate passes that paved way for scores began to develop. Having won senior and minor medals with Ballerin, he won an Ulster junior medal in 1953. Injury had kept him out of the Ulster final. He scored a point in the All-Ireland final and is currently on the county finance committee, and his nephew Enda Gormley was on the 1993 team. Other Mullans, Bobby, James, Gerald, Dermot and Jim, all helped Ballerin score one of the biggest upsets in Derry club championship history when they defeated Jim McKeever's Ballymaguigan by 3-8 to 2-6 in the 1957 county final at Dungiven.

At thirty-two the daddy of the team, goal-scorer Owen Gribben from Newbridge was from another great football family. A farmer, he stood 5 feet 10 and weighed 12 stone 12. He had started playing in Anahorrish school, made his senior debut in 1945, and had a long career interrupted by a broken wrist in a club game. An outstanding midfielder, he also proved an adept centre-half and left-corner back, had many memorable games at centre-forward, and, in the tradition of aging GAA stars, finished his days at full-forward leading the Newbridge attack with his brother Mick. Roddy figured on the substitutes. He played in 1959, and his sons now play for the Newbridge club.

Charlie "Chuck" Higgins played with O'Donovan Rossa. He was twenty-five, at 5 feet 6 the smallest of the team, and weighed 12 stone. He started his football in St Joseph's, Magherafelt, and in his youth was greatly influenced by National League winning players Francie Niblock and Roddy Gribben. He graduated through minor and junior to first team in 1951, featured in the 1954 McKenna Cup win over Armagh in 1954, opted out of football for a few years, and returned in 1957. He was the side's penalty-taker, and in play linked up with Dinny McKeever and Owen Gribben, showing a great ability to put a low ball into the net.

Team manager Roddy Gribben from Newbridge, recovering from injury, is a retired farmer and a regular in attendance at matches and training sessions ever since. Others to feature on the panel were 21-year-old Leo O'Neill and Armagh's 1977 All-Ireland team manager, Gerry O'Neill from Kilrea, both elder brothers of Martin O'Neill, who went on to captain Northern Ireland, play in the World Cup finals, and as manager of Wycombe Wanderers was tipped as a successor to Brian Clough as Nottingham Forest manager in 1993. Colm O'Neill from Draperstown played on until the late 1960s and coached schools teams. Tom Scullion from Bellaghy went on to become manager of Derry's 1987 Ulster championship team. Liam Mulholland from Bellaghy survived to win an All-Ireland club medal in 1971. Joe McCann, a teacher from Bellaghy, was at the end of his career. Séamus Young from Lavey, who died in 1988, was the only one not to survive to see the fulfilment of a dream.

The recollections of Patsy Breen, written many years later, are as good a viewing point for the story of that game as any, for it is in such snapshot vivid recollections that the match lived on wherever Derry football followers talked for four decades. Patsy recalled: "Our dressing-room below the Cusack Stand buzzed with excitement that All-Ireland final day as I somewhat reluctantly went through the old routine of togging out. The scene, I suppose, is typical of that big occasion: jerseys were distributed, officials fussed about as if they were playing, and the embrocation flowed like buttermilk. It was nearly impossible to keep calm under the circumstances. The only thing one could do was to make sure those laces were tied on the outside of the ankles and check on the correct number of folds on the sleeves. At last we filed down the tunnel, groomed to perfection in appearance, and inside tingling with an excitement which is part of what football is all about.

"I knew it was coming; we all knew it was coming, but never in all my experience had we taken the field amidst such a thunder of applause. One moment a foreboding silence, such as might precede the crisis of a great battle, next an uproar of cheering. I closed my eyes and imagined myself among those tumultuous thousands, as I had been in other years. This was different: we were the centre of attraction for cameramen, spectators, Artane Boys, and even for a hovering plane advertising Pak orange.

"The ball was flying high and accurately between the posts before some people had even got to their seats. There were lightning solo runs and elusive body swerves. Derry were playing brilliantly, even better than against Kerry in the semi-final. The first half seemed to go over in a flash as Dublin set the pace and Derry resisted. All the excitement was reserved for the second half, when, amidst unforgettable scenes of jubilation, we drew level. It was, I think, at this stage that we thought we had it and lost our concentration. Then Dublin scored a demoralising goal and it was all over.

"The full-time whistle, I am sure, was sweet music to Des Ferguson's ear, and as I shook hands in congratulation I had one wish and that was to see Derry back again in an All-Ireland in my lifetime. There were so many ready to shake us by the hand and tender loyal sympathy. There were so many glad to greet us now that the battle was over and wish us better luck some other day. All in all it seemed, though beaten, that Derry had at last arrived at a place in the sun."

True, Derry were not up to the task of beating Dublin, but they certainly gave their supporters a game to remember. They entered the field to the most thunderous reception anyone could remember. Spirits were high as "Biddy Mulligan, the Pride of the Coombe" paraded with the Dublin team before the game.

Considering the attempts of his predecessor to wipe out the GAA, it was ironic that when Derry eventually reached the 1958 All-Ireland, the bishop, Buncrana-born St Columb's past president, Neil Farren, threw in the ball, as was GAA practice right up to the 1950s. The bishop's lucky touch kept Derry going for forty minutes. With twenty minutes to go Derry drew level and were still in the hunt. In the manner of so many outsiders before and since, they succumbed to the pressure, to lose by 2-12 to 1-9.

There was enormous good will for this Derry team. Afterwards, some of the supporters were critical of former Cavan player and referee Simon Deignan, some for his unwillingess to play the GAA's admittedly non-existent advantage rule, others for his decision not to award Derry frees for repeated fouls on full-forward Owen Gribben, and the entire population of Derry for his decision not to award what they saw as a certain Derry penalty when the ball was picked off the ground in the Dublin square down under the canal end. That Deignan was related through marriage to one of the Dublin players was enough to arouse such suspicions. To this day, a replay of the game in Derry minds shows that just one or two lucky breaks might have landed Sam back in Maghera instead of Marino.

Derry started the second half reasonably confidently with the wind at their backs and Dublin still within their sights, four points ahead. Dublin's goalkeeper, Paddy O'Flaherty, was forced to make two superb saves from Brendan Murray and Brian Mullan before the veteran on the Derry team, Owen Gribben, set Dublin back on their heels with that goal in the tenth minute of the second half. There were just three points in it and the pressure was on.

For two-and-a-half glorious minutes, Derry were within sight of the Sam Maguire. Dublin switched Lar Foley to midfield to counter McKeever, but when Des Ferguson's centre bounced twenty-five yards from the Derry goal, corner-back Tommy Doherty went to turn, lost his footing, and ended up on his backside. It is a nightmare moment that will live on in his and every Derry man's memory:

73,371 hearts in 73,371 mouths, and Paddy Farnan bearing down on Patsy Gormley in the Derry goal. Stranded, like Niall Glúndubh at the Battle of Islandbridge many Septembers before.

Derry might have coped better with that tragedy, but they didn't. Freaney was allowed to tack on three points, two from needlessly conceded frees, and it was all over bar the shouting when Johnny Joyce finished off a superb move with Ollie Freaney and Jock Haughey, of Swatragh ancestry and a brother of a later Taoiseach, to put the ball in the net off an upright. Peter Smith's and Seán O'Connell's closing points only served to put a respectable look on the scoreboard. Kevin Heffernan captained Dublin and scored three of his side's points. Ollie Freaney scored 0-7, the late Paddy Farnan 1-1, Johnny Joyce 1-0, and John Timmons 0-1.

In choosing a contemporary account to complete the picture of the game, it is natural to use the man who was probably the greatest GAA sports writer of all time. Paddy Mehigan watched the drama from the old press seats in the lower deck of the Cusack Stand, a stand that has now gone, like Paddy himself, to happier places.

Writing under one of his pen-names, "Carbery", he described the day: "The Dublin-Derry senior Gaelic football championship final of 1958 carried all the old final-day glamour. Following a lovely morning—sun and breeze—cloud gathered about noon as I was heading north through Dublin's crowded city for Croke Park Mecca. I had hundreds of fellow pilgrims to accompany me even at that early hour.

1958 All-Ireland final: Derry vs Dublin.
Back row: P. McLarnon, S. O'Connell, H. F. Gribben, P. Breen,
P. Stuart, B. Murray, P. Smith, R. Gribben.
Front row: D. McKeever, B. Mullan, O. Gribben,
J. McKeever (captain), C. Higgins, T. Doherty, C. Mulholland,
P. Gormley.

(Photo: Lensmen)

1958 All-Ireland: Derry vs Dublin.
Patsy Farnan tussles with Tommy Doherty as goalie Patsy
Gormley comes out to clear his lines.

(Photo: Lensmen)

1993 Ulster final: Derry vs Donegal.
The disappointment is over.

(Photo: Sportsfile)

1993 Ulster final: Derry vs Donegal. Joyce McMullan
(Donegal) and Anthony Tohill (Derry).

(Photo: Sportsfile)

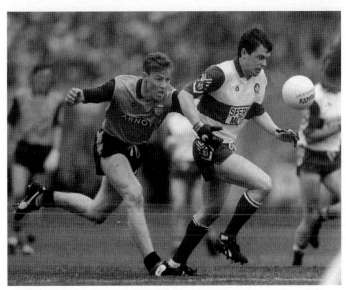

1993 All-Ireland semi-final: Derry vs Dublin. Paul Bealin
(Dublin) and Joe Brolly (Derry).

(Photo: Sportsfile)

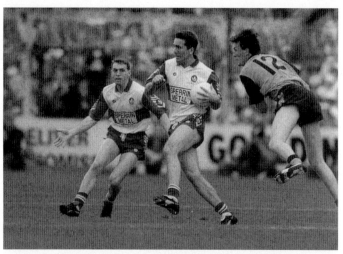

1993 All-Ireland semi-final: Derry vs Dublin.
Veteran of the team Damien Barton crashes through.

(Photo: Sportsfile)

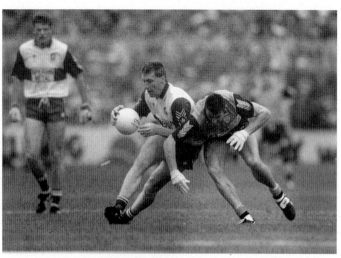

1993 All-Ireland semi-final: Derry vs Dublin.
Brian McGilligan (Derry) and Jack Sheedy (Dublin).

(Photo: Sportsfile)

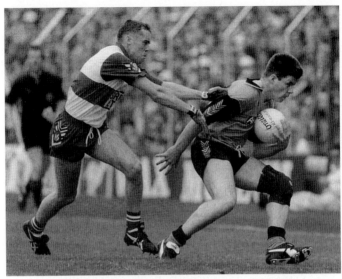

1993 All-Ireland semi-final: Derry vs Dublin.
Gary Coleman (Derry) and Dessie Farrell (Dublin).

(Photo: Sportsfile)

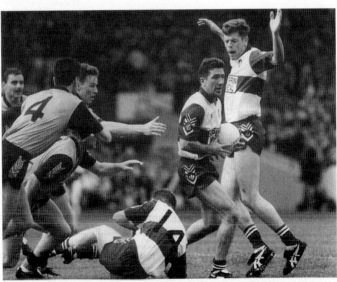

1993 All-Ireland semi-final: Derry vs Dublin.
Paddy Moran (Dublin), Damien Barton (Derry) and Anthony
Tohill (Derry).

(Photo: Sportsfile)

1993 All-Ireland final: Derry vs Cork.
Back row: J. Brolly, D. Heaney, A. Tohill, D. McCusker,
S. Downey, T. Scullion, D. Barton, B. McGilligan.
Front row: E. Gormley, J. McGurk, H. Downey (captain),
K. McKeever, G. Coleman, F. McCusker, D. Cassidy.

(Photo: Sportsfile)

1993 All-Ireland final: Derry vs Cork. Brian McGilligan
(Derry) and Shay Fahy (Cork).

(Photo: Sportsfile).

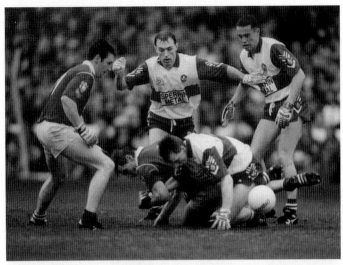

1993 All-Ireland final: Derry vs Cork.
Steven O'Brien (Cork), Henry Downey (Derry) and
Kieran McKeever (Derry).

(Photo: Sportsfile)

1993 All-Ireland final: Derry vs Cork.
Brian McGilligan (Derry) and Teddy McCarthy (Cork).

(Photo: Sportsfile)

1993 All-Ireland final: Derry vs Cork.
Henry Downey (captain) with the Sam Maguire Cup.

(Photo: Sportsfile)

"All we had heard about big crowds expected for the football final was not mythical. The black streams of humanity filled every approaching road. The terraces were rapidly filled and every vantage point—even the roofs of the stands and the long railway wall—had their patiently waiting occupants. Doors and gates were all locked an hour before the senior game opened. It was estimated by Mr Pádraig Ó Caoimh and his officials that about 25,000 people were locked out—73,371 passed through the turnstiles. Skilful stewarding and good humoured crowds helped in the smooth running of a splendid afternoon's sport. Clouds gathered, but the rain held off, and football was good throughout.

"I have heard many thundering receptions for teams entering the playing pitch at Croke Park, but when these red and white clad athletes from Derry pranced in on Sunday, the roofs on the stands shook with the volume of cheering. This was a tribute to the young men from the most historic of our severed six counties. This was Derry's first appearance in Croke Park in a senior championship and the sporting crowds rose to them. They were worthy of the acclaim for they treated the packed and swaying crowds to a sound exhibition of good Gaelic football. They handled high balls with the precision and confidence of a Kerry side and their midfield were masters of every branch of the Gaelic art and their forwards rivalled Dublin in the well-controlled, slick movements near goal.

"Mr Simon Deignan of Cavan's greatest All-Ireland sides is considered one of our very best referees and he never had any trouble with two sporting sides. Dublin won the toss and played into the Railway goal. There was a good steady breeze from the city to aid them.

"What first impressed me was the fine, confident fielding of the ball by Derry backs and midfield. There was no hesitancy here, as was usual with Ulster sides in the past. Gribben, Doherty, McLarnon, Breen and Smith broke up many wind-borne Dublin drives, and I settled down to see a good game of Gaelic football.

"Ollie Freaney's place-kicking was deadly accurate for Dublin and referee Deignan's extra-keen refereeing gave Ollie many extra opportunities. Dublin ran up five points in the first quarter to Derry's two, but there was no evidence yet of defeat or victory, for Derry were standing up in solid phalanx and giving Dublin's scoring machine few open paths to the goal. Seán O'Connell, a tall Derry school-teacher, was the most dangerous of Derry's attackers and he landed two good points in sharp exchange with Dublin's high-over-the-bar scores. With the wind to aid them in the second half Derry were by no means out of it at eight points to four.

"We had a rattling third quarter. Derry's captain, Jim McKeever, hit one of his inspired periods and played havoc in and around midfield. He fielded at all angles and drove beautifully directed balls goalwards; he pointed one and forced a free later which Seán O'Connell pointed and the score read: Dublin 8, Derry 6, and the breeze freshening.

"Dublin got busy then and Haughey's runs held the field; Ollie Freaney pointed (free) and Dublin were again a goal clear. Back came Derry with a rattle, and in swept her forwards. When Owenie Gribben crashed a goal to balance the scores there was a solid roar from the excited Derry (and neutral) followers. Scores were level pegging 0-9 to 1-6.

"We were brimful of incidents now, for Des Ferguson streaked away and swung one across to Farnan on Dublin's right wing—Doherty in checking slipped and Farnan raced through and drove a perfect grounder hard and straight to the net. That was the decisive score. Freaney's points off frees stretched the lead. O'Connell had a fine point for Derry. A beautiful Dublin movement saw Joyce crash Dublin's second goal through and the game was over.

"Derry battled on unperturbed and two points to remind us that these Northmen finished undaunted, finished a solid, if not classic game. Derry will be back again."

The post-mortems continue to this day. Roddy Gribben was team manager. Although in peak condition at the time, he felt that he should have brought himself on, something he was reluctant to do. "John Wilson managed to throw Owen Gribben to the ground every time the ball came near, and we should have changed tactics and drawn him out. When I played full-forward myself I always played out. That was the only way to play Wilson, to play him deep. I know now I should have done that, but we were always waiting to get a foul or a free. A lot of neutrals felt we got a raw deal. That memory of 1958 lived on. It was good to see it buried for once and all in 1993."

The team returned to a fantastic reception from thousands of supporters in Maghera. Cheering crowds gathered at many points along the road. At Dunleer and Dundalk, people had recycled some of their red-and-white flags from Louth's 1957 All-Ireland in honour of the Derry men as they passed through. Just outside Armagh a *Good luck, Derry* red-and-white arch remained standing. At Maghera they were driven around the town. At Fairhill on the outskirts of the town they were given an official reception by Derry County Board and the local Gaelic football club. J. McLoughlin of Derry County Board congratulated the team. The best ever to represent the county, their victory over Kerry had stirred the hearts of all Ireland, never mind Derry. He was pleased to say the team had played as they always had, in a gentlemanly and sporting manner, and were gallant in defeat. The county board staged a céilí to end the evening.

But the old reminders were there. Fans returning from the game were stopped and searched up to three times by armed B Specials after they had crossed the border at Aughnacloy, including local nationalist MP Eddie McAteer. Occupants were ordered out of cars, the vehicles searched, people's pockets and personal correspondence examined. Two youngsters from Ballyshannon and Bundoran were kept overnight in Enniskillen before being released without charge. McAteer, who described the searches as obstructionist and "deliberate baiting of nationalist people", raised the matter in Stormont, to no avail.

5

BREACH OF PROMISE
1958–1968

There were two possible directions that Derry football could go after that audacious display. One was, like Armagh, to collapse and descend back into oblivion. The other was that the honours would flow after such a promising start.

As it happened, the slip-sliding corner-back of 1958 was only the start of the heartbreak. Matches lost through missed penalties, through faulty finishing, through hostile referees and through sheer hard luck prevented Derry Gaelic from taking what many regard as its rightful place at the top.

But the matter was not entirely left up to Derry. Football followers had identified a great football rivalry in the making: and whenever Derry met Down over the next four years, the crowds would flock. After the All-Ireland, Derry beat Down in the Lagan Cup semi-final and went on to win the competition. In the Wembley tournament semi-final, Down won by 2-7 to 1-9.

Roddy Gribben comments: "Down were very good right enough, but we had a very backward-looking county board. The county board would not give up the reins to management. They would not hand over to two or three people. They picked the team. The reading of the official guide was that there would be no committee, including a selection committee, without the county chairman. He didn't think he could delegate power."

Derry showed signs of jitteriness when they lost by 2-5 to 2-4 to Louth at Ballinascreen, but they cantered through their 1958/59 League campaign and qualified for a highly unusual League semi-final against Leitrim. Leitrim had never played in Croke Park in its entire history, and although they had dropped just one point in a group that included Cavan, Longford, Mayo, Meath, and Sligo, they were expected not to last the pace. As happened in the 1959 Connacht final a few months later, Leitrim played herculean stuff until the final quarter, and the sides were level with fourteen minutes to go. Seán O'Connell capitalised on a Hayden mistake for his and his side's second goal, Brian Mullan had the ball in the net again, and Derry won by 3-7 to 1-6.

This set up Kerry and Derry for a repeat of 1958's seismic semi-final, and this time two first-half goals within a minute of each other from Jim Brosnan and Tom Long ensured that Kerry commanded the entire affair, Derry's only heroics coming in the final quarter when they managed to get an eight-point margin back to three, eventually losing by 2-8 to 1-8. Owen Gribben had punched the goal that restored contact, but the attendance of 32,405 indicated that Derry people did not expect much from the encounter anyway.

P. Gormley; P. McLarnon, H. F. Gribben, T. Doherty; P. Breen, C. Mulholland, P. Smith, J. McKeever, L. O'Neill; S. O'Connell, B. Murray, D. McKeever; B. Mullan, O. Gribben, P. Stuart.

Bellaghy had been the dominant team in the Derry club championship for three decades, since the 1950s brought about the transformation of the Derry championship. Until 1957 Derry's three divisional champions qualified for the county championship play-offs with the City, North and South winners alternately given a bye into the final.

Seán O'Connell explains the spirit of Derry club football. "Loyalty is exhibited in a lifelong dedication to a club, and it is a loyalty based far more on giving than on taking. You can see it in all the varied and ongoing voluntary work, the improvement in facilities, the management of teams, administration, fund-raising, making refreshments for club functions—all giving scope to young and old, rich and poor, strong or feeble."

For years, far away from the glamour of Croke Park, thousands of hours had been spent collecting money, building club-houses, washing jerseys, making tea, and turning in hours of playing time for the great Derry clubs: Ballerin, Ballinascreen, Ballinderry, Banagher, Bellaghy Wolfe Tones, Castledawson, Craigbane, Desertmartin St Martin's, Dungiven St Patrick's, Glack, Glen, Kilrea Pearses, Lavey Erin's Own, Magherafelt O'Donovan Rossas, Newbridge, Slaughtneil Emmets, Swatragh.

Not all of these teams got their names on the Derry championship honours list. Ballinascreen, the home parish of Ulster Council delegate Michael Collins, won three titles between 1934 and 1941. In 1937 Newbridge won the championship on objection after Lavey had won what would have been their first title on the field. In 1938 Lavey won the title, and, counting the objection year, took four football and two hurling titles in a seven-year period with such as Éamonn Diamond, John Fay, Hugh McGurk, Hugh A. McGurk, Tony McGurk, John Francis O'Neill and Joe O'Neill on the team.

In 1939 Magherafelt won the championship in their first appearance in twelve years, beating Dungiven in the final, and went on to win four titles in a ten-year period. The 1942 final had the unusual occurrence of the county secretary, Paddy McFlynn, being sent off by the county chairman, Paddy Larkin. As he was suspended from all GAA activity, he would sit outside the meeting in another room, and from time to time members would leave the room to consult him.

In 1947 Dungiven won the title for the first time, defeating Lavey with a superb goal from Charlie Hasson. Derry city took their last title in 1952 when Éire Óg surprised Desertmartin in the final by 1-2 to 1-0. In 1953 Desertmartin defeated Ballerin by a record nineteen points, 4-10 to 0-2, on a day on which nine of the Ballerin players had played in the county minor final, staged as a curtain-raiser before the football game. In 1954 Lavey re-emerged, with Pat McCloy and Murty Higgins on the team.

Bellaghy club had been founded after a discussion between Edward Scullion, Hugh McGoldrick and two others at McNicholl's corner in the town in the 1930s, and for a period in their colourful early history players from the Ballyscullion end of the parish used boats to cross the river. They toiled away in obscurity until, scarcely noticed, they won the Derry minor league and successive championships. In 1951 Bellaghy defeated Newbridge but were easily beaten by Dungiven in their first county final. Harry Cassidy managed the 1956 team that made the breakthrough, beating Drum in the county final. Local people remember this as the year when the town's new hall was opened, they arrived on the football map, and somehow things fell into place. In the next sixteen years, Bellaghy were to run up twelve Derry titles, a run that culminated in their becoming the second All-Ireland club champions in 1972.

There was a major upset in 1957 when Seán O'Connell, Brian Mullan and Brendan Murray helped Ballerin to defeat Bellaghy's conquerors, Jim McKeever's big, strong Ballymaguigan side, by 3-8 to 2-6 in the 1957 county final at Dungiven on 13 October. Seán O'Connell and Michael Mullan countered McKeever at midfield. Patsy Mullan scored two goals within a minute of each other in the first half, and the match was sealed by a third from Brian Mullan after Ballymaguigan had come back with a Barney Rea penalty. Ballymaguigan had to wait until 1962 for their first county title, when Éamonn Coleman helped them beat Castledawson in a replay. Bellaghy, Ballinderry, Ballerin and Lavey dominated the later championships, all of them winning Ulster titles, while Dungiven also took four titles between 1983 and 1991.

It was in the League that Derry showed their first signs of taking up where they had left off in 1958. They defeated Down and qualified for the 1958/59 semi-final; Seán O'Connell set Phil Stuart up for a late winning point against Mayo, 0-11 to 1-7, and all was set for another showdown with Kerry.

Twenty-point defeats don't happen very often in major finals. Perhaps Kerry felt they still had to exorcise the ghosts of 1958, and the result was the most one-sided League final in twenty-five years, since Fermanagh had been humbled by the might of Mayo in the 1930s. Derry had an early goal disallowed because it was thrown to the net, and had to wait nineteen minutes for their first score. They still trailed by just two points at half time, 0-8 to 1-3, thanks to a Denis McKeever goal, and the 32,254 attendance braced itself for an exciting second half. All the excitement was at one end, and most of it came in the first six minutes after the break: John Dowling had a goal almost from the throw-in, O'Dowd had a goal, McAuliffe had two points, and O'Dowd had another goal. The score was 3-10 to 1-3, and Kerry were out of sight.

Nevertheless, this was only Derry's third League final team: P. Gormley; P. McLarnon, B. Devlin, H. F. Gribben; C. Mulholland, T. Scullion, P. Smith; P. Stuart, B. Murray; Jim McKeever, Seán O'Connell, L. O'Neill; D. McKeever, W. O'Kane, C. O'Connor. Substitutes: G. Magee (C. O'Connor), G. O'Neill (Stuart), C. O'Connor (Gormley).

The Ulster brew had served up exciting Tyrone, Derry and Down teams in quick succession.

Was this the Armagh team that had come so close to history in 1953? By 1959 they seemed to have fallen right out of the Ulster equation, and then suddenly, on the last day of May 1959, Derry were counting the cost of taking them for granted. Derry were missing Patsy Gormley, Seán O'Connell and Phil Stuart as they set out in defence of their title. This was a desperately hard-fought match, coming just three weeks after the League final, full of holding and jersey-pulling and petty animosities. Derry had the wind in the first half, but for eight minutes they hadn't even got a wide to their name. In the Armagh midfield John McGeary and Gene Larkin outplayed the heroic Jim McKeever. Then Eddie O'Neill pounced for an Armagh goal two minutes before half time. It was 1-1 to 0-3 at the break, 1-6 to 0-5 at the end, and only five thousand turned out to see yesterday's heroes humiliated. Armagh people still remember that championship with some frustration. For a short period after J. Brady scored a winning goal for Cavan against Derry's conquerors in the Ulster semi-final the umpire behind the goal tried unsuccessfully to signal to the referee that there were three men in the Armagh square.

Derry waited twelve months for the chance to resolve that argument with Armagh at Magherafelt, and when the teams met on 5 June 1960 it could not have been against a more dramatic backdrop. Jim McKeever started at centre-half-forward but when he switched to centrefield was again the hero. With Derry winning by 3-10 to 1-9 the storm began, thunder, lightning and Big Jim competing for the attention of the soaking spectators.

But Derry were in difficulties right from the start of their Ulster semi-final against Cavan; they trailed 2-3 to 0-2 at half time and lost by 3-6 to 0-5 before a smallish eight thousand crowd, thanks to two goals from Seán Conaty and one from Jim Sheridan. Phil Stuart and Dermot Mullan were both injured for this game, but Pete Smith had

returned and Derry had few excuses. It was little consolation for Derry that they reversed the result, beating Cavan
by 2-5 to 1-5 in the 1960 McKenna Cup final six weeks
later, on 28 August, the day that Ballinascreen's Dean
McGlinchey Park was reopened.

Derry qualified for the 1961 Ulster semi-final with a 2-10 to
0-4 win over Donegal at Ballybofey, and a slightly more
hair-raising two-point win over Tyrone at Ballinascreen,
1-9 to 0-10, thanks to a goal from substitute Séamus Devlin
after twelve minutes.

Down and Derry's rivalry had come of age. When the
teams met in the McKenna Cup semi-final, fifteen
thousand turned up to watch. That was just short of the
eighteen thousand who came to Casement Park to see their
meeting in the 1961 Ulster semi-final, the first in the
championship since the 1958 final. Jarlath Carey had
perhaps his best match ever in the Down jersey at
Casement Park. Jim McCartan and Paddy Doherty got the
goals that kept Down on course for three in a row in Ulster.
Derry went out by 2-12 to 1-10.

Derry lost that match—regarded still as one of the best
in the entire history of the Ulster championship—by five
points. Their supporters had many incidents, perhaps too
many, on which to reflect. After seven minutes, Derry led
by a point. After twenty-six minutes of the second half
there were three points between the sides. Then their best
chance came from Leo O'Neill five minutes from the end,
when he shot wide from just inside the Down square. Their
only goal came when Dinny McKeever's cross was flicked

to the net by Brian Rafferty. According to John D. Hickey in the *Irish Independent*, "so fast and furious was this battle royal, played in ideal conditions before an attendance of 18,000, that I could not believe the hour had sped when Liam Maguire whistled the end of play. That whistle was the only discordant note of an hour that was so captivating that one could not avoid taking sides now and then. Even those with no affinity whatever with either side must have found enchantment in a game that was contested with an intense fervour, frequently with some superb individual efforts and some brilliantly conceived combined movements, all of which were provided by the winners who showed their real worth when their peril was great, as often it was in a titanic second half. While Down deserved their triumph, if for no other reason than they fought back like real champions, after they had been pummelled by a Derry transformed by the switch of Jim McKeever from the forty to midfield, my one regret at the end of the hour was that it did not end with honours even. The pace from start to finish, the hard knocks that were given and taken in the pursuit of victory but in no spirit of rancour, the sheer brilliance of Jarlath Carey, the splendour of Tony Hadden's every move, Derry's heroic fight-back through most of the second half and the titanic finish of Down made it an hour that will live in my memory for many a long day.

"In view of Derry's feeble effort against Kerry in the League final some may say that the Mourne county men beat nothing, but the Derry of yesterday and the Derry of the league decider, believe me, were poles apart."

In 1962 Derry brought in newcomers Denis Cassidy, Brian Rafferty and Jackie McNally to restore their fortunes. They made heavy work of beating Donegal by 2-10 to 2-7 before a puny three thousand attendance at Magherafelt, and they might have lost their semi-final at wind and rain-lashed Dungannon to Tyrone by ten points rather than four, 1-9 to 2-2, were it not for two goals in the dying minutes. Jim McKeever had moved from centre-half-forward to midfield. After twenty-six minutes the Tyrone defenders dropped a greasy ball and Seán O'Connell seized the moment for a goal, and in lost time Brian Devlin scored the second. Derry were missing Hugh Francis Gribben and George McGee, and trailed by 0-5 to 0-1 after a thoroughly miserable first half.

Things could hardly get worse, but they did. In 1963 Derry lost their proud ten-year unbeaten record at Ballinascreen when they lost the first round of the Ulster championship to Cavan, 3-9 to 2-8. That year's absentees were goalkeeper Seán McGuigan and midfielder George McGee, but Jim McKeever was talked into playing, and Liam McIldowney and Brian Rafferty returned for the game. But Derry's chances evaporated when Leo O'Neill missed three sparkling chances. In the very first minute he was wide when he could have fisted an early goal; after fifteen minutes he shot wide when he was inside the square; and just after half time Cavan goalkeeper Seán Flood saved magnificently from O'Neill's third chance. At half time it was 2-7 to 0-3, and the match was long out of reach when Seán O'Connell and Denis McKeever eventually got Derry's goals.

The following year, on a dangerous pitch resembling a

skating rink in the eyes of one commentator, Cavan won again by 3-9 to 2-3 before two thousand dedicated followers. This could not have been further removed from the glamour of Croke Park. The match started twenty-seven minutes late, and was over at half time when Cavan led by 1-3 to 0-2; Derry's two well-worked goals, from McGuigan and Rafferty in the second half, were both greatly helped by conditions. The 21-year-old Éamonn McCann from Castledawson was the championship newcomer, Derry having avoided the temptation to pick Ulster championship winning juniors such as Frank O'Loane and Larry Diamond, keeping them for the All-Ireland series. As it happened, Derry were beaten 2-12 to 2-8 by Meath in the first All-Ireland semi-final to be staged at Ballinascreen, on 16 August of that year, but their Ulster final victory over Antrim, 2-13 to 0-8, was the cause of much-needed celebration. It was classic junior fare, a mixture of players on the way up and others on the way down. Frank O'Loane scored 0-5, Phil Stuart 1-2, Larry Diamond, and Willie Strathead. But the significance of that achievement would be dwarfed by the minors of a year later.

Larry Diamond, Frank Connolly and Ted McCloskey, goalkeeper Michael Ryan from Lissan, Frank Lagan and Frank Kelly joined the team for the 1965 campaign, when even lowly Antrim got in on the act, beating Derry with two goals from twenty-year-old Michael McRory at Ballinascreen. Charlie O'Connor was recalled for this game, but Jim McKeever, in the twilight of his career, opted to go to New York rather than stage another comeback. Derry's selectors switched their players round repeatedly to try to get a foothold on the game, and only goalkeeper Michael Ran and midfielder Larry Diamond finished in their original positions.

Having lost three successive first-round ties for the first time since 1950, Derry appeared to do a little better against Antrim at Casement Park in 1966. They were level four times in the first half but failed to score at all in the second half, and lost by 2-7 to 0-6. They anxiously promoted two eighteen-year-olds, Mickey Niblock and J. J. Kearney, to that team; for the first time, members of the Derry fifteen had All-Ireland medals to show for their efforts.

For much of the history of the Ulster minor football championship, Derry had not bothered to enter. Later GAA president Paddy McFlynn was on the first Derry team to compete, in 1936, when training consisted of early morning runs around Ballyheifer led by a boxer, P. J. Robinson. They had never contested a provincial final at this level, leaving Antrim, Armagh and Tyrone to pick up the spoils instead. The year 1965 could not have been more different: Derry romped through Ulster and captured the All-Ireland title.

They had telegraphed their intentions early in the year: St Columb's won their first All-Ireland colleges title under the stewardship of former Fermanagh player Ignatius McQuillan in April 1965. Seven of that team were eligible for Derry minors, and Tommy Quinn, Michael P. Kelly, Colm Mullan, Malachy McAfee, Séamus Lagan, Brendan Molloy and poc fada champion Philip Friel all trained on in Derry during the summer.

A second party trained at Ballinascreen, where special

lighting was installed for training purposes, under county player Seán O'Connell, and the two came together at weekends for team practice. The team had qualified for the All-Ireland final when two decisive changes were made: Eugene McCaul of Foreglen was placed in goal, and the multi-purpose Friel was brought in to the forwards. Both played important parts in a decisive victory over hot favourites Kerry in the final.

Derry fell four points to one behind before coming back to 0-3 to 0-4 at half time. Then came Friel's switch from left to right corner. McCaul saved three certain Kerry goals. After nineteen minutes of the second half Kerry had a soft goal when McCaul let a forty-yard lob from a Fergus Moroney free crash into the net. A minute later Friel stabbed the ball past the Kerry goalkeeper from close range. After twenty-eight minutes Brian McCarthy had a Kerry goal. Friel fetched Malachy McAfee's lob, cut in swiftly, his rising shot was parried by the Kerry goalkeeper and came back into the path of Séamus McCloskey. The net rattled, Derry won their first All-Ireland at any level, and the minor title went north for the first time since Armagh's 1949 victory.

Dónal Carroll wrote in the *Irish Independent*: "Dapper Derry are the 1965 All-Ireland minor champions and right well do they deserve the honour. Playing in their first decider, they not only ruffled famed Kerry out of their normally fluid approach but also captivated the huge headquarters attendance by producing most of the good football in a hard, rather than spectacular encounter. Coming from behind to win by 2-8 to 2-4, Kerry had only one score, a goal, from play. Derry's was a team success for in the swaying fortunes of this game every sector was tried sorely but emerged with greatly enhanced reputations. The first half was poor enough, with too much spoiling to permit open play, and too little thought in deliveries to initiate any movements worthy of note."

Those history-making minors were: E. McCaul; A. Burke, T. Quinn, M. Kelly; C. Mullan, C. McAfee, A. McGuckian; T. Diamond, S. Lagan; B. Mullan, M. Niblock, E. Coleman; S. Kearney, S. McCluskey, P. Friel.

While the seniors continued to lose, other Derry teams came close to success. In 1966 Derry reached the Ulster minor football final again but this time succumbed to Down, 1-12 to 1-9. Derry won the Ulster junior championship for 1967 as well, defeating Cavan by 2-8 to 0-4 in Coalisland on 28 May. On 13 August Mayo ended their run with a 0-12 to 1-4 win in the All-Ireland semi-final at Castlebar. There was hope once more.

6

CONTROVERSY AND CHAMPIONSHIPS
1968–1978

When Derry met Down in the 1967 championship at
Newry, three players were booked and a newspaper
commented that tackling was hard all through. The game
was unremarkable, unless one counts two goals from
fourteen-yard frees, one from Seán O'Connell in the third
minute and another from Down's John Murphy eight
minutes into the second half; and its story was best
summed up by the statistics of the first quarter: Derry had
five wides, Down scored four points. Down won by 3-9 to
1-10, but few among the attendance noticed the grudges
that were bubbling away between the respective players.

Derry were already known as a physical team, but the
first-round tie between Down and Derry on 9 June 1968
went into history for all the wrong reasons. In the first
eleven minutes of play Derry conceded nine frees, and were
accused of using their elbows indiscriminately as play
progressed. To the modern spectator, the total of forty-five
frees is not high (a stoppage every eighty seconds compares
almost exactly to the drawn match between the same
teams in 1991), but there was an outcry after the game.
Derry conceded 29 of these frees, 17 in the first half, and
Down just 16 in all. Four players were sent off, Down's
John Murphy and Derry's Tommy Diamond after forty
minutes and Down's Ray McConville and Derry's Mickey

Niblock later in the game, and one reporter claimed that the entire Derry team were lucky to stay on the field. Derry felt they should have won that match. Instead Down went on to win an All-Ireland.

Scores were level three times in the first half. Down led 0-5 to 0-4 at half time, Down had a goal from Seán O'Neill in the first half, and Derry's goal from Séamus Lagan came too late to affect the outcome of the game. Down won by 1-8 to 1-6 and went on to win the All-Ireland. The "Battle of Ballinascreen" became the subject of an Ulster Council investigation. Derry supporters still find it hard to credit. "Ridiculous," says 1947 captain Pat Keenan. "It was a good match. It wasn't bad." Roddy Gribben felt it was just tension that caused the trouble. "Ballinascreen is a small pitch and the crowd are right in on the players. The press went to town on it."

There was much excitement over the new under-21 championship in the mid-1960s. Early winners of the competition rejoiced that success was automatically around the corner: Kildare in 1965, Roscommon in 1966, promoting teams wholesale and folding their arms waiting for the cupboard to fill up.

Derry waited for the 1965 minors to filter through before swooping on the Ulster under-21 title in 1967, beating Monaghan by 1-11 to 1-4 on 30 July in Dungannon for their first Ulster title. But the journey to Charlestown for an All-Ireland semi-final on 27 August against Mayo brought no joy, as Mayo won by 3-9 to 1-8.

That strengthened their resolve for the 1968 campaign.

Derry beat Donegal by 2-10 to 0-3, Tyrone by 3-6 to 1-4, Down by 0-10 to 0-7, and Monaghan by 4-9 to 2-4 in the Ulster final.

In the All-Ireland semi-final they led Kerry by seven points at half time of their tie on 25 August at Ballinascreen, but Kerry fought back to within a point in the second half. A 44th-minute goal by Kevin Teague set Derry back on course for a 2-11 to 0-10 victory.

Derry's first All-Ireland title in this grade was achieved on 8 September 1968. It was all effectively over at half time. Offaly were reduced to fourteen men five minutes before the interval, and Derry led by 1-5 to 0-2 at the break, thanks to a glorious fisted goal from Séamus McCloskey. A pinpoint shot by Mickey Niblock and a third goal from Éamonn Coleman wrapped up the title in the second half. Despite the award of 22 frees to Derry and 38 to Offaly, the match had its free-flowing periods, but referee Jim Hatton was escorted to the dressing-room amid some cat-calling from Offaly fans. The powerful physique, fitness and superb teamwork of the Derry men was commented upon by the spectators. Gay Crehan scored 1-8 of Offaly's total. Derry 3-9, Offaly 1-9.

The All-Ireland under-21 champions' team was J. Somers; M. Trolan, T. Quinn, M. P. Kelly; T. Diamond, M. McAfee, G. O'Loughlin; T. McGuinness, S. Lagan; E. Coleman, M. Niblock, J. J. Kearney; A. McGuickian, S. McCluskey, K. Teague. Substitutes: A. McGurk, C. O'Donnell.

Derry promoted five of the under-21 team for the 1969 Ulster championship, defeating Tyrone by 2-8 to 0-8 with two Colm McGuigan goals at Dungannon. Derry trailed by a point for much of the match, a game memorable for Derry's comeback in the final seven minutes.

Derry had never drawn a championship match when their match against Cavan at Clones on 29 June 1969 finished level. Derry appeared to throw away their chance by shooting eleven wides in the first half, but when they brought Seán O'Connell on eight minutes into the second half they looked set for victory until a speculative lob by Gallagher was bundled into the net by Phil Murray for Cavan's second goal ten minutes from the end. Cavan won the replay by 1-8 to 0-6, Cusack getting the goal in the first half and Derry paying the price of shooting eighteen wides and losing out at midfield. Inaccuracy was to cost them many a match during those frustrating early 1970s.

Derry reached the 1968 Ulster minor final but were well beaten by Armagh, 4-8 to 1-7. In 1969 they signalled their intentions by beating Monaghan by 1-17 to 1-6 in the Ulster minor league final, and raced through their campaign, beating Down by 5-10 to 0-1, Antrim by 3-7 to 1-4, Tyrone by 1-9 to 0-5 and Wexford by 0-14 to 3-4 to reach their second All-Ireland minor final. This time they lost to Cork.

The star of the 1970 Derry minor team was Martin O'Neill, who featured on the St Malachy's team beaten by a last-minute goal in a classic All-Ireland colleges final the previous April. With Liam O'Hara, Maurice Brennan, and Mark McFeeley, Derry won the Ulster minor title again, beating Down by 7-9 to 0-4 at Newry, Tyrone by 2-11 to 0-6 at Ballybofey, and surprise packets Fermanagh, winners of the Ulster minor league, by 1-14 to 0-11 at Clones. By 2-10 to 0-11 Kerry put them out of the All-Ireland championship.

The All-Ireland final team was: K. McGahon; P. Burke, L. Murphy, P. McGuckian; B. Kearney, M. Moran, R. Hasson; E. Lavery, H. McGoldrick; S. Mullan, B. Ward, T. McWilliams; M. O'Neill, S. McGeehan, G. O'Neill. Substitutes: M. Bradley, S. Coyle.

The juniors defeated Tyrone by 1-4 to 0-5, Donegal by 3-9 to 1-8, Cavan by 2-11 to 1-8 after a 2-5 draw and Down by 4-9 to 2-5 before going down to Kerry in an All-Ireland semi-final in Tralee on 3 August, 0-12 to 1-4.

Gaelic football had changed dramatically over a three-year period. The old leather football, which became unplayable in wet weather, was replaced with a ball that was coated in plastic. Boots were getting lighter. Small rural clubs were appointing team coaches, experiments with direct pick-up and thirteen-a-side games were taking place, and in 1970 the playing time for provincial finals and the All-Ireland series was extended by twenty minutes.

Whether the playing of the first eighty-minute Ulster final in 1970 benefited Derry was never quite resolved. Derry entered with a strong squad, beaten by Mayo in a disappointing National League semi-final. The League campaign had begun well but a poor performance in a divisional play-off, beating Sligo by 1-11 to 1-7 in Bally-shannon, did not augur well for the closing stages of the League. But Derry had scored 14 goals and 89 points in seven matches in the first half of the year, including a 6-8 to 1-4 victory over Mayo in a challenge match in Crossmolina in January.

Crossmolina in January should not be taken as a guide to subsequent events in 1970, but already the Derry qualities could be seen: superb physical fitness and a towering physique. Only Éamonn Coleman and Gerry O'Loughlin of that team were under six feet. A League title would have done the emerging 1965 and 1968 minors no harm at all to blood them for a decade at the top.

Instead Mayo won the semi-final when Derry's equalising point was disallowed in a bizarre sequence of events. As full time approached, Mickey Niblock was hauled down approaching the goal, Seán O'Connell took the free, which he chipped in to the goalmouth, Séamus Lagan punched it over the bar, and Derry were half through their sigh of relief when referee Jim Hatton indicated that Mayo had won the match by a point. The game was over, and he extended it to allow the free to be taken, he told O'Connell, but O'Connell chased him as far as the dressing-room to remonstrate: he should have been told and he would have attempted to put it over the bar. He had no case. There was nothing in the rule book to compel a referee to tell a free-kicker that this was the last kick of the match, although courtesy had long dictated that this was the practice.

On to the championship, and an undaunting home tie against Tyrone at Ballinascreen. Derry started with a point and a goal in the first minute, a Séamus Lagan lob that caught out the goalkeeper; Seán O'Connell sent a penalty in after fifteen minutes, and Hugh Niblock finished the best move of the match eight minutes from the end. Con Kenneally reported: "Derry looked anything but provincial champions when they trounced Tyrone 3-12 to 0-7 in the Ulster championship at Ballinascreen. What Derry would have done to the losers had they a full side—they were short the Diamond brothers and Mickey Niblock with Malachy McAfee out through injury, but playing in the second half—can only be a matter of conjecture. They were never in the slightest danger of losing this rough and tumble encounter. It got a little too rough towards the end and referee Liam Maguire ordered the loser's right corner back to the line. At this stage the game was as good as over and the heavy tackling, especially by the Tyrone backs, was pointless."

On to Irvinestown and an even rougher match. Cavan recalled Jimmy Stafford for his first championship match since 1964. Derry went 1-3 to nil up after sixteen minutes, thanks to a Mickey Niblock goal, and under siege at the end brought Séamus Lagan back to midfield from corner-forward. Derry 1-8, Cavan 1-5. John D. Hickey reported: "The game had nothing to recommend it as apart from the liberties players were allowed in the employment of strong-arm tactics it was a scrambling affair in which Derry failed to live up to promise. Much of a contest that was a travesty of the code was positively dangerous to limb if not life and it baffled me that referee Tommy Johnston of Fermanagh did no more than take a few names or wave an admonishing finger at gladiators who obviously were prepared to adopt any methods in the pursuit of victory. If the conduct that we saw, tripping, hacking, elbowing, charges of malicious intent and even pulling down by the neck goes without rebuke because the referee failed to exercise his authority, the powers that be will be shirking their responsibility. Brain, it is sad to say was utterly subordinated to brawn, the hour disgraceful because of all the reprehensible acts we saw which did no credit to either side or to the association. In my opinion it was so offensive that it seems to be an obligation on the Ulster council to hold an investigation into the whole sorry affair."

Since 1958 Down and Cavan had dominated the Ulster championship. The 1970 finalists offered at least a change of scenery. Star of Antrim's under-21 success in 1969, Aidan Hamill, proved to be the find of the Ulster championship. The twenty-year-old scored two goals against Monaghan to earn Antrim's place in the final. Antrim's team was small of stature: against the likes of 6 feet 2 Larry Diamond and 6 feet 3 Séamus Lagan they would have their work cut out for them. Lagan and Diamond obliterated the Antrim midfield, Derry scored five points in the first five minutes, Seán O'Connell took Séamus Lagan's centre for a goal after twenty-two minutes, and Lagan added another just before half time. The half-time lead of 2-9 to 0-6 was reduced to four points, but Derry's fitness told in the extra twenty minutes. A goal from Tony McAtamney in the final minute helped dress up the scoreline: Derry 2-13, Antrim 1-12, and the Ulster title back in Derry for the second time.

Penalties featured strongly in Derry's 1970 championship campaign, one scored by Seán O'Connell and missed by a Tyrone man in the first round, another first-half penalty taken by Antrim's Aidan Hamill saved against the post by Séamus Hasson in the Ulster final, and, tragically, two missed by Derry men in the All-Ireland semi-final. It was a technique that Gaelic players in general were finding difficult to master: in that championship just three of the nine penalties awarded ended up in the net.

There was a dramatic first quarter. While Kerry's masseur, Owen McCrohan, frantically tended the thigh of injured Mick O'Connell on the sideline, Derry showed great promise and were leading by 0-5 to 0-2 when the first free was awarded for a foul on Brian Devlin after twenty-one minutes of the first half. Seán O'Connell's feeble kick was easily saved by Johnny Culloty. Eight minutes into the second half Derry led by 0-9 to 0-8 when Seán O'Connell was pulled down. He ignored calls to come up to take a second, Séamus Lagan took it instead and sent it harmlessly wide. Eight minutes after half time the sides were level; after ten minutes Kerry had taken the lead, and after seventy minutes Kerry were leading 0-14 to 0-9 when Derry's heads dropped. They eventually lost by a humiliating thirteen points, at least one newspaper reporting that their physical advantages had become an encumbrance to Derry. Kerry 0-23, Derry 0-10, a day to be forgotten.

Despite their being installed as 3-to-1 joint favourites with Down to retain the Ulster title, Derry's supporters scarcely took an interest in their bid to defend that hard won Ulster title. Just three thousand showed up the following 6 June to see Derry beat Fermanagh by 4-10 to 1-10 in Ballinascreen, Niblock, McGurk, Brian Devlin and Niblock again scoring the goals. At Casement Park four thousand watched Derry's pedestrian 0-8 to 0-4 win over Antrim in a repeat of the previous year's Ulster final. Against Down in the last Ulster final to be played at Casement Park, about twenty thousand showed up.

Down won a tremendously exciting Ulster final by four points, 4-15 to 4-11, one of the best. Seán O'Neill laid on goals for John Murphy and Michael Cunningham in the first half. Michael Cunningham and Dónal Davey struck twice more in the second half, and then Mickey Niblock brought Derry storming back with left and right-footed goals.

Derry completed a McKenna Cup three-in-a-row in 1971: on 15 June 1969 Derry beat Tyrone 0-14 to 0-8 in Casement Park; Derry beat Down 0-10 to 1-4 in Casement Park; on 12 September 1971 Derry beat Down by 3-6 to 1-8 in Dungannon. Down prevented four in a row with a 2-13 to 1-6 win in the 1972 final at Dungannon.

The under-21s defeated Armagh by 2-11 to 2-4 and Antrim by 3-10 to 1-3 to reach the 1972 Ulster final. There they were held to a draw by Tyrone, 1-7 each, and roundly defeated in the replay, 3-13 to 1-7.

If a Derry club was to win an All-Ireland championship, it was fitting that Bellaghy should do it. Since that sudden 1956 breakthrough they had claimed the Derry championship as their own. The abolition of the inter-district competition in 1957 seemed to release them from perennial clashes with Ballymaguigan, and they won eleven out of fourteen titles, a procession of victories that other clubs envied. Tom Scullion's total of eleven Derry senior championship medals may never be beaten.

Between 1963 and 1965 Bellaghy defeated Ballerin in three successive finals. Newbridge stole the crown away from them in 1966, 1967, and 1970. Club members backboned the Derry teams of the 1960s. Tommy Diamond became the first Derry man to captain Derry All-Ireland winning teams at two grades, 1965 minor and 1968 under-21. Their 1971 victory over Lavey by 2-12 to 0-5 qualified them for the 1972 club football championship. In what was only the second year of the competition, Bellaghy defeated Armagh's Clan na nGael by 1-11 to 0-5 six days before Christmas 1971 in Dungannon. They got a home tie against Portlaoise in the All-Ireland semi-final the following April, winning by 1-11 to 1-10 in Magherafelt.

It was on a Friday evening (throw-in 7:30) in a draughty and eerily empty Croke Park two days before the National Football League final that Bellaghy made their piece of history.

When Bellaghy defeated UCC by a single point, 0-15 to 1-11, in the All-Ireland final in Croke Park on 12 May it proved an exciting game for the handful of spectators. Bellaghy used the wind to take a 0-8 to 0-5 half-time lead, Dónal Kavanagh scored an equalising goal for the students thirteen minutes into the second half, the sides were level five times in all, and Bellaghy fought from behind for their win when Frankie O'Loane pointed a free and Brendan Kavanagh sent the winning point spinning in off the post. O'Loane scored seven points in all, five from frees; Tom Scullion, Hugh McGoldrick, Frank Cassidy and Larry Diamond all did their bit. The ankle injury that might keep Brendan Lynch out of Kerry's League final was the talking

point in the following morning's newspapers. In vain
Bellaghy waited for the cup. As happened with Pat Keenan
after the 1947 National Football League final, there was no
cup, nor any official to present it. Nobody had bothered to
have it returned from the previous winners, East Kerry. In
future years, when club championships rival the National
League in importance and attract crowds of fifty thousand
to their finals, they will marvel at such disrespect.

Bellaghy's winning team was: Patsy McTaggart; Tom
Scullion, Austin Mulholland, Frank Cassidy; Tommy
Diamond, Hugh McGoldrick, Chris Browne; Larry Diamond,
Peter Doherty; Francis Downey, Brendan Cassidy, Frankie
O'Loane; Hugh Donnelly, Tom Quinn, Kevin Cassidy.

Derry's 1972 championship bid seemed to be going well by
mid-summer. In the first round they hammered five goals
past Fermanagh, two from Hugh Niblock and one each
from Adrian McGuckian, Larry Diamond, and Anthony
McGurk. In the quarter-final they recovered from the set-
back of first-half Antrim goals by P. J. O'Hare and Adrian
Hamill, regained their composure, and Hugh Niblock took
Larry Diamond's pass for a first goal after forty minutes and
shot four points in the last seven minutes.

That should have been warning enough, but there was
shock all round when Tyrone's collection of Vocational
Schools and minors promoted to the senior team shocked
the fancied Derry team by 1-8 to 0-9 in O'Neill Park,
Dungannon. With the wind in the first half, Derry were too
casual, and then their 0 6 to 0 3 lead disappeared when
Frank Quinn got a Tyrone goal half a minute before the

interval. With fourteen minutes to go, Tyrone took the lead and were leading by three points with eight minutes to go as punches began to fly and Derry's patience wore thin. Three Tyrone players and two Derry men were booked.

It was in the League that Derry found fortune with a remarkable run between 1970 and 1976. Finishing with three wins, three draws, and one defeat in the 1970/71 League, Derry had to beat Antrim by 1-7 to 1-6 to qualify for the semi-final.

As it happened, Kerry seemed to choose the League to exorcise the ghost of Seán O'Connell's 1958 semi-final strike. A win by 3-10 to 2-7 in a New Eltham tournament final in 1971 over a team that had only five of Kerry's All-Ireland selection was small compensation for the series of two League semi-final defeats and a controversial withdrawal that Derry suffered at the hands of Kerry between 1970/71 and 1972/73.

Derry needed a Johnny O'Leary goal to get a narrow-squeak win over Antrim and qualify for the first and closest, played on 16 May 1971. It ended in a one-point defeat by 1-11 to 1-10 that might have been a very different match had not the Derry goalkeeper turned the ball into his own net in the seventh minute. An Anthony McGurk goal brought the margin back to two points; with six minutes to go it was three points, and two points from Seán O'Connell closed it to one before the final whistle. Larry Diamond played an inspirational game, and Derry regretted the loss of Malachy McAfee, injured early in the game but carrying on ineffectively.

In the 1971/72 League Derry had maximum points from their seven matches in Division 1B, beating Antrim, Down, Fermanagh, Laois, Mayo, Meath, and Sligo. Derry's second League semi-final of 9 April 1972 against Kerry was regarded as too physical, and the teams were level six times in the first half and eight times in all before three Kerry points in as many minutes mid-way through the second half gave them the leeway they needed. Seán O'Connell scored six points and John O'Leary three as Derry went out of the semi-final by four points.

Derry's League semi-final teams were:

1971: Séamus Hasson, Tom Quinn, H. Diamond, Matt Trolan, Hugh Niblock, Malachy McAfee, Gerry O'Loughlin, Larry Diamond, A. McGuckian, Seán O'Connell, Anthony McGurk, Éamonn Coleman, B. Ward, S. Gribben, John O'Leary. Substitute: Peter Stevenson (McAfee).

1972: John Somers, Matt Trolan, Tom Quinn, M. Kelly, C. Browne, Hugh McGoldrick, Gerry O'Loughlin, Larry Diamond, Tom McGuinness, Anthony McGurk, Colm P. Mullan, Éamonn Coleman, Adrian McGuckian, Seán O'Connell, John O'Leary. Substitutes: Malachy McAfee for McGoldrick, Mickey Moran for McGurk.

In a period of thirty-two months Derry had suffered four heavy defeats to Kerry, an All-Ireland and League semi-final, and a grounds tournament tie, enjoying only an unremarkable win before a few hundred spectators in that New Eltham tournament game over a team that contained just five of Kerry's first choice fifteen.

When they faced Kerry in the semi-final of the 1972/73

National Football League, they might have good reason to be pleased with the result: a 2-5 to 0-11 draw. In fact the result of that 1973 semi-final is largely forgotten, lost in the war that broke out between Derry and the GAA hierarchy. Now largely forgotten, the repercussions for the GAA in Derry were immense, as the county withdrew from the semi-final replay at short notice, fought against a fine and suspensions imposed by the Activities Committee, and ended up tamely bowing out of the 1973 championship.

The decision of referee Paul Kelly to disallow a Derry goal a minute before half time, then to send off two Derry men within two minutes of each other mid-way through the second half, raised the ire of Derry players and supporters alike.

Derry finished top of Division 1B that year, suffering just one defeat in seven matches. In the final they had been playing well: Anthony McGurk had robbed goalkeeper Éamonn Fitzgerald for a first goal after twelve minutes, and McGurk was put through by Mickey Niblock five minutes before half time for the second. They led by two points, 2-4 to 0-8, when the players were sent off but were running out of steam and had to rely on a plethora of professional fouls and Kerry missing chances in the closing minutes to keep their noses in the game.

Inefficient stewarding of the sideline seats meant that matters were likely to get out of hand as the final whistle approached and a couple of hundred unruly Derry supporters spilled on to the sidelines. When referee Kelly tried to leave the field, he ran into a full Foyle-fired fury: "They came at me like wild animals," he said, visibly shaken in the dressing-room afterwards, and he had to be saved from a serious assault by the Gardaí. One garda was taken to hospital having been slashed with a bottle, others were kicked and punched; bottles, soft drink cans and pieces of the seats, ripped out from the concrete, were hurled down on the gardaí from the Hogan stand, and newspaper headlines the following day declared it the Battle of Croke Park. Two Derry men, one from Swatragh and one from Dungiven, ended up in court the following day. Derry County Board deplored the actions of their so-called followers. They soon had good reason to. There were strong suggestions that the riot was inspired by Derry's infamous physical tactics. John D. Hickey reported: "Derry players and believe me far more than a few of them used most reprehensible tactics right from the start. Fists and elbows were used indiscriminately. Their tackling often suggested that many of them thought they were engaged in a rugby game rather than a Gaelic football match, and they were adept in the employment of the trip. No one can say with conviction why Kerry did not win and even made such hard work of earning a draw in view of their marked numerical superiority for so long. My opinion, and it is tendered after mature consideration, is that the Kerrymen, and rightly so, were more concerned about their personal safety than they were perturbed about the possibility of defeat. Derry supporters could assert that some of their players were the victims of acts which should not be seen on any sportsfield. They were. But the Kerry violations of the canons of good sportsmanship did not erupt until their patience, quite obviously and understandably, had been exhausted."

There was general expectation that Derry would be accorded the blame for the fracas and severely punished. A Kerry official told Hickey: "Unless the right tail is pinned on the right ass, should there be any soft-pedalling, we will have a lot to say." It was clear that Derry had a lot of work on its hands dissociating what they regarded as their legitimate physical tactics on the field from the after-match riot. After a lengthy meeting in Ballinascreen on the Wednesday after the match, Derry secretary Pat Mullan issued a statement. "As far as the incidents after the match are concerned, the board condemns and deplores them without reservation," but refused to comment on "the match itself and the referee's report," as they "are still sub judice."

Derry wanted to go further. They argued that the Activities Committee inquiry into the incidents, fixed for 19 April, should be postponed to allow passions to die down. They also sought a guarantee that "the game be divorced from all other issues" (for which read the riot), requested that RTE videotape of the game be made available, asked that no Derry players be asked to make personal statements that would "in any way reflect on the reputation of a fellow Gaelic sportsman," and called for the inquiry to be conducted at a pace that would give time to parties to present their case. "Any haste which might be prejudicial to anyone's case must be avoided." They also asked that the inquiry be public and that the media have access to all aspects of its working, and reserved the right to comment on the referee's performance in a subsequent report to the inquiry.

All of these demands were rejected, and on 19 April the Activities Committee fined Derry £500 for the riot and suspended the two players who had been sent off.

But Derry's disappointment at these decisions paled beside the indignation with which they discovered that Paul Kelly had been appointed to referee the replay. Derry delegates believed that the very presence of Paul Kelly at the replay would be enough to cause another riot. As one newspaper put it delicately, "Derry representatives painted frightening pictures of what people with no connection whatsoever with Gaelic affairs might do if the Dublin referee was in charge of the replay."

Five Derry delegates—Francie Donaghy, Séamus and Pat Mullan, John McCrystal, and Jack MacAuley—failed to show up at the GAA congress in Waterford, although Tommy Mellon, Hugh Carey and John McGlinchey did show up. County chairman Pat Breen theorised that it was a personal reaction on the part of the five not to turn up. There was widespread speculation that Derry would pull out of the replay.

Behind the scenes things were looking considerably brighter. The newly elected president of the GAA made three telephone calls to Patsy Breen, indicating that Paul Kelly could be asked to step down. Two members of the county board were also given the impression by two members of the Activities Committee that John Moloney would be brought in to referee the second game. A meeting at Bellaghy on 24 April went on into the early hours as Derry discussed their strategy. It was decided to appeal against the fines and suspensions, and to accept the concession they believed they had been granted on the issue of the referee.

On Wednesday morning Breen told the newspapers: "We have decided to turn up, okay; but did we ever say we would not? A statement has been sent on to Croke Park, and the full details of our meeting have been described." Mullan said that the only statement he would be making to Croke Park "would be to say that the Derry team to meet Kerry was being picked on Wednesday night following a training session in Ballinascreen. Last night's meeting could not have gone more smoothly, and everyone was in agreement that we play the game. There was never any question of us pulling out, and we are treating the match like any other."

All Derry's appeals were rejected at a prolonged meeting in Croke Park on 27 April. Breen stormed out of the meeting, telephoned team manager Harry Cassidy, and issued a statement that the team would not travel. He had not consulted his colleagues on the county board, but nobody was going to publicly repudiate his sentiments. A statement from Derry County Board on 29 April said: "The decision arrived at in Croke Park at 2 a.m. on Saturday re their withdrawal from the game with Kerry was reached in all good faith even though there were divergent views as to whether or not it was right. The board agrees that the delegates were put in an invidious position when, our appeals having been rejected, it was announced there would be no change of referee. Regardless of any personal feelings, the board abides by the decision." Mullan complained that "in the face of the greatest provocation they had tried to keep the whole affair in a low key but they felt it was now time that the facts were presented to the public and particularly to their own supporters."

Derry went so far as to appoint a sub-committee to draw up a comprehensive document on the whole affair. Their 27-page report was released at a press conference in the Wolfe Tone Social Centre, Bellaghy, on Monday 18 June, containing photocopies of all the letters that passed between Croke Park and the board. The report

— dissociated Derry from the after-match riot, and "unreservedly condemned the actions of a small group of alleged supporters";

— claimed that any attempt at impartiality was avoided in the after-match hysteria, with the game not being divorced from the incidents at the end;

— asserted that Derry had been pilloried while no blame was attached to any other party;

— expressed alarm at the undue haste with which the inquiry by the Activities Committee was rushed;

— revealed that two suspended Derry players were ordered out of the precincts of the Croke Park office area while awaiting the decision of their cases; and

— pointed out that, even after the Activities Committee had found the GAA's Management Committee responsible for the security at Croke Park, still fined Derry £500 for the riot, and assured Derry they would not be fined if there was another riot at the replay.

County chairman Patsy Breen said the report was issued "so we could get back on the rails to express to everyone how we were treated, to hope that something similar would not happen to another county." He said, "We would like the friendships to be maintained, but we must state that before the match we were given assurances that we would not have the same referee as in the first match."

Tommy Mellon, Liam Hinphy, Séamus Mullan, John McGlinchey and Pat Mullan said that the Activities Committee, under Noel Drumgoole, had at first accepted a proposal that Derry be put out of the National League. "They were going to put us out, but there was a bit of stocktaking done. They counted up the cost of not having the replay, added on the £500, and decided it would not be better. The ideals and principles of the association were not to be found at the fore of some minds at that time. The study group felt there was too much haste by the Activities Committee to get the investigation over and done with and they did not try to divorce the after-match scenes from the actual game."

Liam Hinphy added: "One would expect from an organisation such as ours decent standards, but what was being conducted was a kangaroo court. There can be double standards anywhere, but we feel that this is so in the GAA. Even in our own case the rules changed. We were fined £500, mainly because of the trouble at the end of the first game, but then we were told that we would not be responsible if the same thing happened at the end of the second match. The Derry County Board is not responsible for Croke Park security. The Derry board has no intention of paying the £500 fine but they expect that it will be taken from their share of the National League proceeds. They had donations from friends throughout the country, including some county boards, to offset the loss from this fine." Breen said: "It was a bad night when they fined us and suspended two of our players, but Croke Park acted dictatorially by naming Paul Kelly as referee for the replay on the same night."

The players too were disaffected. On 27 May the players issued a statement before the challenge match against Kildare at Naas, expressing "grave dissatisfaction with the Activities Committee as a result of the Derry-Kerry match. Seán O'Connell has given a great service to the GAA and to Derry in particular, and we feel it was extremely vindictive to suspend a player indefinitely on the allegations of Tom Prendergast. Seán O'Connell is beyond reproach as a sportsman, and we have never known him to have his name taken or to be suspended. We greatly believe that the GAA has been greatly degraded when one player informs on another. Signed: Gerry O'Loughlin, Adrian McGuckian, Pat Doherty, Francis Moran, Hugh McGoldrick, Fintan McCloskey, Liam McGurk, Tony Moran, Matt Trolan, Mick McGuckian, Tom McGuinness, Laurence Diamond, Malachy McAfee, Frankie O'Loane, John Somers, Séamus Regan, Hughie Niblock, Matthew McGurk, Pearce Mellon, Harry Cassidy (team manager), Harry Gribben (selector)."

For a time it looked as if O'Connell would never play football again. He had no intention of appearing before the Activities Committee, who suspended him until he appeared before them. Kerry's Tom Prendergast was given a two-month suspension for allegedly striking Gerry O'Loughlin during the game. The Kerry man mentioned

O'Connell in his relation of the game, but it was claimed at the June press conference that O'Connell, who was not present, had "no intention of being a clashback." Derry's report on the affair stated: "No Derry player is prepared to make statements which could in any way damage the reputation of a fellow Gaelic sportsman." Tommy Mellon queried the principle of whether or not a player must appear before a disciplinary committee at a Central Council meeting. Sports writer John D. Hickey opined that "with O'Connell Derry have got themselves into a blind alley." O'Connell himself was in hospital in Coleraine with a stomach complaint and was due to be operated on the following Wednesday.

Such high dander was taking its toll. Derry were beaten 3-15 to 4-8 in that challenge. When the championship opened, Mick and Hugh Niblock were in the United States, Tom Quinn and Chris Browne were suspended, Malachy McAfee had lost interest, O'Connell was suffering from the dual impediment of injury and suspension, and Éamonn Coleman and Frank O'Loane were also missed from the team. Despite this, newcomer John O'Leary scored a magnificent goal to help them beat Monaghan by 1-7 to 0-4, and there were three debutants—James Convery, Jude Hargan, and Seán Donaghy—on the team that was beaten by Down in the Ulster semi-final.

Down led by 0-5 to 0-1 after nine minutes but Derry fed the ball low in to full-forward Peter Doherty and came back to 0-7 each at half time, and Down wrapped up their place in the Ulster final with a goal from Eugene Cole with six minutes to go to the final whistle. Gerry Forrest did hit the post as Derry attacked at the end, but it was a sorry end to a season that had promised so much.

The bitterness took many years to subside. Jim McKeever wrote in the programme for the opening of Cumber Field in Claudy that "it is a really impressive display of the true quality of Gaelic sport in the county which would be much more worthy of the attention of the Dublin mass-media than the few peccadilloes on which they have gorged themselves in their cannibalistic treatment of Derry in recent years."

The team that played and nearly beat Kerry, who went on to win their third successive League title, on that infamous semi-final day in Croke Park in 1973 deserves its place in Derry history. It can be entered in the record, not so much as a near-miss but as an unfinished episode. The fifteen were: John Somers; Matt Trolan, Séamus Lagan, Adrian McGuckian, Chris Browne, Mick McGuckian, Gerry O'Loughlin, Larry Diamond, Tom McGuinness, Peter Doherty, Malachy McAfee, Tom Quinn, Anthony McGurk, Mickey Niblock, Frank O'Loane. Substitutes: Seán O'Connell for O'Loane, John O'Leary for Doherty. John O'Leary and Eugene Laverty were selected to replace the two suspended players in the replay.

Derry's defeats against Down in the 1973 and 1974 championships were comprehensive, the second salvage-able until twelve minutes from the end, when Seán O'Neill drew the goalkeeper before flicking the ball over John Somers's head, 1-12 to 0-7. By way of compensation, Derry beat Monaghan by 4-5 to 2-10 at Monaghan to win the

McKenna Cup for the fifth time on 8 September 1974. Derry missed the 1973/74 League semi-final by two points, finishing with four wins and three defeats in Division 1B.

If Derry feel bad about a 1975 championship run that could have gone better, pity poor Monaghan. After a poor display against Armagh had yielded an eleven-point victory in Omagh, Derry faced Monaghan for the third championship in succession. Derry trailed by three points as time ticked away. Then Eugene Laverty was fouled in the last minute, and Peter Stevenson coolly sent goalkeeper Paul McCarthy the wrong way. Monaghan did everything right in the replay and led by six points after eighteen minutes, and this despite Ciarán Finlay missing a Monaghan penalty. Derry moved Gerry McElhinney to midfield and had equalised with fifteen minutes to go, and went on to win by fourteen points to 1-6.

After that near-miss, manager Frankie Kearney was elated. "Our young players can handle anything." Although nobody outside the county believed it, he was right. "It was a game befitting the occasion," said the *Irish Times*. A drama-charged encounter won with an impressive degree of conviction by newly vibrant Derry. "A lot of hearts, guts and determination" was Peter Stevenson's verdict on the day. Just three minutes into the game Seán O'Connell set up eighteen-year-old Gerry McElhinney for the first goal, Derry led 1-5 to 1-3 at half time, and Down missed a penalty as Derry kept their nerve in the second half. Mickey Lynch and Seán O'Connell scored five points each, while Down's two goals by Willie Walsh came too late to make a difference. Tom McGuinness outfielded the

Down midfielders, and Derry were in an All-Ireland semi-final against Dublin.

Although young, the team had no shortage of credentials. John Somers was Ulster reserve goalkeeper. Liam Murphy had captained Queen's 1971 Sigerson-winning fifteen. Tom Quinn had already won four All-Ireland medals with St Colum's, Derry minors, Derry under-21s, and Bellaghy. Peter Stevenson was also a St Colum's 1965 man, and an Ulster Railway Cup hurler, no less. Anthony McGurk won an All-Star award in 1974 and 1976, a Sigerson medal with Queen's in 1971, and a Railway Cup medal with the universities in 1973. Gerry O'Loughlin and Tom McGuinness had played Railway Cup football with Ulster. Mickey Lynch won man of the match in the Ulster final. Johnny O'Leary had played alongside Pat O'Neill and David Hickey at UCD. Mickey Moran and Brendan Kelly had emerged from the relatively new GAA nursery of St Patrick's, Maghera. Seán O'Connell had been to the All-Ireland before, in 1958. The man who proved to be the best prospect of them all, Gerry McElhinney, was just eighteen, already an accomplished Ulster champion boxer, and had made his debut in the McKenna Cup campaign. Liam Murphy was injured three nights before the Ulster final.

Derry seized a surprise 2-2 to 0-6 lead but crumbled to a five-point defeat, Dublin 3-13, Derry 3-8, and many agreed with Derry captain Peter Stevenson when he maintained that Dublin were not five points the better team. Veteran Seán O'Connell and John O'Leary scored the first two goals, and an inconsequential third goal followed from

Brendan Kelly, three minutes from the end. Dublin goals from Anton O'Toole in the thirty-third and sixty-third minutes and Tony Hanahoe in the forty-sixth minute effectively kept the game out of Derry's reach.

Although crowd trouble spoiled the semi-final, Derry fans escaped blame this time as Dublin's trouble-makers among the 44,455 attendance took centre stage themselves. The minor match between Kildare and Tyrone was held up for five minutes, a youth was stabbed, three gardaí injured, a Cavan priest had his face slashed, scores of bottles were flung onto the field, and questions were asked why there were only thirty-five gardaí on duty in the ground.

Kevin Heffernan declared: "We did not know what to expect. They played some great football, and our experience pulled us through. It was harder than I had thought it might be, but we were never taking anything for granted." Jimmy Keaveney commented that Derry's football was good, open football; "they never looked like falling apart and kept coming back at us." A disappointed Francie Donaghy commented: "Dublin just deserved it, but we'll be back." They were indeed back to face Dublin in Croke Park again, sooner than they thought.

Derry's 1975/76 League campaign started with two satisfactory wins, a 0-14 to 0-9 victory over Tyrone at Dungannon and a win over Sligo by 0-16 to 0-2 at Ballymote. But it was a 2-12 to 0-2 win over the previous year's National League champions, Meath, at Ballinascreen on 23 November that suddenly set the team alight; and although they were beaten by Galway in Tuam they finished with a win over Mayo to tie with Galway at the top of their division. They won a divisional play-off against Galway by 2-11 to 2-6, and went to Croke Park on 11 April and beat Cork by a point in an exciting semi-final, Derry 1-7, Cork 1-6, thanks to a Mark McFeeley save in the very last minute of play. Derry shot eight wides in the first half of this match, having succumbed to a third-minute goal from Jimmy Barry Murphy, and a punched goal from Seán O'Connell put them in the driving seat from half time on.

An RTE television strike did not noticeably swell the attendance for the League final, 33,845 to see Dublin repeat their 1975 All-Ireland semi-final victory over Derry by a single point, 2-10 to 0-15. Dublin won with the help of two dodgy goals, both involving a push in the build-up. Derry were leading by 0-9 to 0-4 when Pat Gogarty scored a goal just before half time. After forty-four minutes Gay O'Driscoll, Dave Hickey and Tony Hanahoe were involved in the build-up for a goal by Keaveney. It was still level after forty-nine minutes, thanks to points from Mickey Lynch and Brendan Kelly, and might have been level again at the end had Robbie Kelleher not broken up Derry's last attack.

Derry's League final team was: Mark McFeeley, Liam Murphy, Tom Quinn, Peter Stevenson, Gerry O'Loughlin, Anthony McGurk, Mickey Moran, Tom McGuinness, Séamus Lagan, Gerry McElhinney, Mickey Lynch, Gabriel Bradley, B. Kelly, Seán O'Connell, John O'Leary. Substitutes: F. McCloskey for Lagan, A. McGuckian for Bradley.

Derry were to be the last team in Ulster to successfully defend the provincial title. Their run to the 1976 final was hardly memorable; the clash with Armagh in Omagh was one of the most disappointing in years; and although Tyrone hauled their arrears back to one point with five minutes to go they never looked like contenders. Then when everything looked reasonably relaxed Derry's Ulster final against Cavan in 1976 turned into a bit of an endurance test. Brendan Kelly, Johnny O'Leary and Mickey Lynch got the points in the closing stages of extra time after an enthralling replay that contrasted with the rugged draw between the same teams. Cavan's John Dwyer had stalled the Derry celebrations with an equalising point that forced the replay to extra time. He had earlier got Cavan's goal in the tenth minute. Derry's John O'Leary and Cavan's Steve Duggan exchanged goals the first day, when Duggan got the equalising point for Cavan. But despite these vital scores Duggan was not quite as impressive as he had been in Cavan's semi-final victory over Down, when he gave a memorable display, or in Cavan's repeat victory over Donegal.

Derry, strangely enough, went comfortably ahead of the defending All-Ireland champions, Mick O'Dwyer's young Kerry lions, and still led by 0-9 to 0-8 at half time in the All-Ireland semi-final. Thereafter their collapse was total. Pat Spillane was felled off the ball when Derry led 0-6 to 0-2, and angered Kerry brought the score back to 0-6 each. Derry regained the initiative, but when super-sub Seán Walsh arrived in the second half the goals began to flow. Four minutes after half time Walsh laid on a goal for Mikey Sheehy. He did it again after forty-nine minutes. Sheehy scored his third after sixty minutes when the goalkeeper parried a Mickey O'Sullivan shot, and Ger O'Driscoll and Seán Walsh got two more goals in the following two minutes. Derry's hero was Gerry McElhinney, whose first-half display caused so much trouble for Kerry. Paddy Downey commented in the *Irish Times*: "When all due credit has been accorded to Kerry, one important fact must be recorded. Derry, who dictated the trend of play through the greater part of the first half, did not deserve to lose by a margin of 16 points." This was Derry's heaviest ever All-Ireland semi-final defeat: 5-14 to 1-10, before an attendance of 30,963.

Parallel with the successful seniors, Derry under-21s eventually won their second Ulster title, defeating Tyrone by 1-11 to 0-10, Donegal by 0-10 to 0-7, and Down in a low-scoring final by 1-6 to 1-4. A trip to Newbridge to meet Kildare ended in defeat, 2-12 to 1-10. There had been some close misses in the meantime. The under-21 team of 1972 had been very unlucky in not taking the Ulster title. They drew the final 1-7 each with Tyrone, but went down spectacularly in the reply: 3-13 to 1-6. Defeated by Tyrone in 1973, Fermanagh in 1974, and Tyrone in 1975. But Dublin and Kerry too had a supply of young players to sustain their success. There was to be no let-up for this Derry team.

7

SWALLOWLESS SUMMERS
1978–1990

Nobody is sure exactly how the three-in-a-row came unstuck in 1977. Tremendous football was played in Derry's defeats of Cavan and Down on the way to the Ulster final. Then, in the final, breakdown. Derry decided not to bring Mickey Moran home from the United States for the final. Armagh took the Ulster title after twenty-four years. The game turned on two spectacular goals in a sixty-second spell before half time. Paddy Moriarty and Noel Marley were the scorers, and Jimmy Kearins wrapped up the argument eight minutes into the second half. With Tom McCreesh outstanding in the Armagh defence, the Derry attack never got going.

Free-scoring matches against Donegal and Tyrone in the 1978 championship had Derry's hopes of a recovery going again, but Jude Hargan's and B. O'Neill's goals proved to be of little use as Derry crashed out of the 1978 Ulster semi-final to Down at Casement Park, 1-14 to 2-8.

The story of Derry's pulsating 2-12 to 1-13 Ulster quarter-final tie against Cavan in 1979 bears retelling. Derry trailed by 0-5 to nil before James McAfee scored their first point from a free in the twentieth minute. A free from James McAfee rebounded off an upright, Eugene Young fisted the ball across the goalmouth, and Brendan Kelly shot to the net to make it 1-3 to 0-8 at half time. Six minutes after half time the sides were level, Derry took the lead, James McAfee scored a goal, and Alfie Dallas put Derry five points up. Now it was Cavan's turn; they started to come back, and Tony Brady scored an equalising goal. The lead changed hands twice more. Tom McGuinness gave Derry the lead twenty-eight minutes into the second half, and Eugene Young and Brendan Kelly points put the match out of Cavan's reach. After all that excitement, Séamus Flynn and Eugene Sharkey scored the goals that helped Donegal oust Derry by 2-9 to 0-14 at Omagh, despite six points from Brendan Kelly.

A year later they made one of the unluckiest championship exits in Derry football history. Against Cavan at Ballinascreen, Anthony McGurk, Gerry McElhinney, Mickey Moran et al. totally dominated the game in the second half, but they let Cavan off the hook, running up seven wides in sixteen minutes. Hugh McGoldrick and Gerry McElhinney contrived to put Colm McKee through for a goal after seventeen minutes of the first half. After half time Moran played as a utility player in midfield, originating some marvellous attacking moves and scoring a second goal. With just thirteen minutes to go Derry still managed to lead by four points after a great solo point by Gerry McElhinney, but things went rapidly awry. Paddy McNamee, who had pounced on a blunder by Derry's goalkeeper in the first half, picked up a through ball from Brian O'Grady and shot to the corner of the net, with eight minutes to go, Cavan revived. Fionán McDonagh scored an equaliser, and Seán Cole and McNamee scored sickening winning points to put Cavan through: Cavan 2-9, Derry 2-7.

The midfield dominance of Tom Doherty helped Derry past Fermanagh, 0-12 to 0-10, in the 1981 championship, despite a heart-stopping near miss by Fermanagh in the closing minutes. Derry had Sligo Rovers soccer star Jim McGroarty and Ulster rugby interprovincial Mark McFeeley in action for this match. That earned a trip to Clones and another chance to experiment with their Down bogey and the boy wonder of Ulster football, Greg Blayney. Down won by twelve points to nine. More summer woe.

The seven thousand fans at Clones that day could dispense with the sorrows of the seniors in the light of the county's minor performance. Trailing at half time by 2-6 to nil, they came back in the second half to win by 3-6 to 2-8, an astonishing performance, the likes of which no-one can remember seeing before or since.

These were bountiful days for Derry minor teams, as when the decade changed, so did the sphere of influence over the Ulster minor championship, away from Tyrone and back north of the Sperrins again to Derry. Derry's record in the 1980s at under-18 level was truly astounding: five titles in seven years of pilgrimage to Clones. They beat Armagh in the 1980 Ulster final and went on to an All-Ireland final against Kerry, losing by 3-12 to 0-11. A 1981 team built around fifteen year old Dermot McNicholl, Danny O'Kane, Liam McElhinney and Eunan Rafferty repeated that Ulster final win over Armagh and defeated Dublin by two points in the All-Ireland semi-final, only to go down by 4-9 to 2-7 against Cork men such as Anthony Davis, Niall Cahalane, Colm O'Neill, John Cleary, and Tony O'Sullivan. Derry tried their comeback heroics against Down again in 1982, Danny O'Kane snatching a late equaliser in the Ulster semi-final before they succumbed in the replay. But it was a temporary aberration. Derry cantered through the Ulster champion-ship, beating Cavan by 5-7 to 2-9, Tyrone by 3-12 to 1-8, Down by 3-2 to 1-6, Monaghan in a one-sided Ulster final by 3-9 to 0-4, and Galway in the All-Ireland semi-final.

Damien Cassidy, nephew of 1958 hero and later team manager Harry, scored 5-10 in that campaign. He and Johnny McGurk were to learn all about beating Cork in an All-Ireland final at an early age.

Dermot McNicholl, who played minor four years in all, captained that team of 1983, when in heavy wind and rain Derry got revenge (Michael Maguire was the only survivor on the Cork team) by 0-8 to 1-3. It was a close call. Bradley conceded a penalty for a foul on Martin Kelleher, and Teddy McCarthy hit a rattling penalty that Don Kelly saved not once but twice, from the rebound as well. Dónal Keenan reported: "Certainly the weather was an influencing factor but it cannot totally be blamed for such a disappointing hour. Despite all that it was a triumph for the Derry team management and for team captain Dermot McNicholl. He was one of the few individuals who lifted this game out of the ashes of disaster." John McGurk recalls: "The conditions were terrible, very hard for minors to play, because the wind was very strong and so I think the bigger players came out tops. I have good memories of winning it. I remember it was a good defensive display, because I think they scored 1-3, which is four scores over sixty minutes."

The 1980 minor team was: J. Mackle; Brian McNabb,

M. O'Brien, Martin Tully; M. Convery, O. McKee, D. McCluskey; Damien Barton, Danny O'Kane; Liam McEllhinney, B. McErlean, John McErlean; P. McKiernan, Terence McGuckian, R. McCusker. Substitutes: M. Bradley, D. McNicholl.

The 1981 team was: Liam Peoples; Brian McNabb, Kevin Rafferty, Éamonn Reilly; Cathal Kelly, Brendan McPeake, Martin Tully; Liam McElhinney, Matt Bradley; Eunan Rafferty, Danny O'Kane, Terence McGuckian; Dermot McNicholl, John McErlean, John A. Mullan. Substitutes: James McGrath, Paul McCormack.

The 1983 team was: Don Kelly; Patrick O'Donnell, Paul Bradley, John McGurk, Raymond Conway, Brian Kealey, Niall Mullan; Peter Young, Ciarán Barton; Cathal McNicholl, Dermot McNicholl, Eddie McElhinney; Éamonn Lynch, Damien Cassidy, Tony McKiernan.

That Fermanagh fright of 1981 was remembered in Irvinestown for twelve months. In 1982 Arthur Mulligan emerged from the second division of the Fermanagh county league to shoot the winning goal that put Derry out of the Ulster quarter-final, Fermanagh's first victory over Derry in the championship. Derry whittled away at Fermanagh's lead throughout the game but succumbed to Dominic Corrigan's winning point at the end to lose by 1-9 to 1-8.

Despite the boost of a win over Dublin, later to be crowned All-Ireland champions that year, at Bellaghy in February 1983, Derry had a miserable league season and began a morale-sapping descent from Division 1 to 3 of the National Football League. Damien Barton scored five

points and full-forward McCusker the goal that day. In the
championship, just three thousand turned out to watch
Cavan, who had not won a championship match since
beating Derry at the same ground three years earlier, win
by 1-12 to 0-11 in the rain at Ballinascreen in 1983 after the
sides were level four times in the second half.

Where the minors had succeeded the under-21s were next
in line. As Donegal cantered to under-21 success in 1982,
they defeated Derry by 0-10 to 1-5 in the Ulster final. In
1983 Derry got revenge, a whopping 3-13 to 1-5 victory
over the reigning champions and a third Ulster championship at this level.

Derry went on to the All-Ireland under-21 final, drawing
with Mayo in one of the wettest games in the history of
this championship in Carrick-on-Shannon. Mayo won the
replay by 1-8 to 1-5.

The 1985 under-21s renewed their 1982 and 1983
acquaintance with Cork. This time Cork won, by 0-14 to
1-8. Derry met Donegal in the 1986 Ulster under-21 final
and won by a convincing 4-7 to 0-6. On a Saturday evening
in Parnell Park, Derry lost the under-21 semi-final again.

The 1983 under-21s defeated by Mayo in the All-Ireland
final were: J. Mackle; K. Rafferty, F. Burke, T. Scullion, John
McErlean, B. McPeake, C. Keenan, C. Quinn, Damien
Barton, Liam McElhinney, Dermot McNicholl, P. McGann,
T. McGuinness, R. McCusker, T. McGuckian. Substitutes:
Danny O'Kane, M. Tully, E. Cassidy. E. Cassidy and B.
McErlean played in the drawn match. Substitutes in the
draw: R. McCusker, P. McCann.

The 1985 under-21s beaten by Cork in the All-Ireland final were: Damien McCusker; Barry Young, Francis Burke, Paul McCann; John McGurk, Brendan McPeake, Niall Mullan; Danny O'Kane, Brian Kealey; Declan McNicholl, Damien Cassidy, Michael McGurk; Dermot McNicholl, Cathal McNicholl, Tony McKiernan. Substitutes: Paul Bradley, Ciarán Barton.

The Centenary Cup of 1984 was the watershed that helped Meath to join the Gaelic elite. It so easily might have done the same for Derry.

Derry had had a wretched League campaign and needed the sort of boost that their seven points to six first-round victory over Cork gave them. The news was even better from then on: another one-point win, 2-11 to 1-13, against Kerry, and a 3-10 to 0-6 quarter-final win over surprise quarter-finalists Wicklow. Derry were eventually beaten by 22 points to 2-11 by Monaghan in the semi-final.

It seemed as if all the commemorative point-kicking and under-age euphoria was eventually having an effect on the seniors when Derry beat Cavan in the 1984 championship, Gabriel Bradley scoring the winning goal six minutes from the end in the sunshine at Breffni Park. Two weeks later at Ballinascreen the sun stayed out but Derry's dreams went abruptly back in: Tyrone 1-13, Derry 3-4. Kevin McCabe, who reeled in the new Derry danger-man Dermot McNicholl, and goal-scorer Damien O'Hagan, were the heroes instead of the McNicholls and Cassidys.

If the Centenary Cup might have been a watershed of sorts, the 1985 open draw was another. After Derry failed to win promotion from Division 3 of the National Football League, a sense of disenchantment with the team management developed among the panel. Tom Scullion, a headmaster in Castledawson, and Chris Browne, a PE teacher in Claudy, took charge of the team on a temporary basis, basically because nobody else was willing to do it. In one of those fits of pique that regularly invade GAA dressing-rooms, five players withdrew from the county squad, and only nine of the twenty-six confirmed that they would travel to Askeaton for the first round of the open draw competition, "a Mickey Mouse competition" in some eyes. There Derry lost heavily to Limerick by ten points to four—lowly Limerick, who a year earlier had been rated as the 31st-best football county in Ireland, ahead of Kilkenny.

John McGurk was supposed to be on that team in Askeaton. "I didn't play. I had a club match that day and I was asked to play, and the rest of them weren't showing so it was a bad occasion." Goalkeeper Damien McCusker was still at school at the time. He thinks the school team was playing that Saturday, so he wasn't able to go down to the game. Lucky.

The team was: J. Mackle, H. McGurk, B. McPeake, T. Scullion, D. McMurray, C. Keenan, M. Tully, J. Irwin, B. McGilligan, B. Murphy, B. Kealy, P. Murphy, C. Faulkner, T. Doherty, E. Donnelly.

When the despair was almost complete, and Derry were quoted at 14 to 1 for the 1985 Ulster title, it all appeared to be coming together at last. Admittedly the penalty that snatched victory from Tyrone in the first round at Ballinascreen was a controversial one, leading to an assault on Cavan referee Michael Greenan by an angry mob of Tyrone supporters after the game. Tyrone were leading by two points when Tommy Doherty caught a sideline kick from Damien Barton and was fouled on the edge of the square, and Declan McNicholl put the penalty away while Tyrone men howled derision at Derry man and referee alike. That was two minutes before the end of normal time, and the referee allowed five more minutes of injury time before Derry scraped through by 1-9 to 1-8. "Larceny!" cried the sports writers. Derry didn't dawdle. They beat Cavan by eleven points to seven at Armagh.

But Derry's final performance was dismal. Having taken control of the match mid-way through the first half, when Éamonn McEneaney fisted the first of his two goals, Monaghan could afford to go twenty-three minutes without a score in the second half as Derry developed stage fright. In the first half Derry had nine wides, Monaghan three, and eventually Derry failed by 2-9 to 0-8. There were no complaints, at least north of the Sperrins.

South of Gallion, they still had spent twelve months saying prayers for Michael Greenan and plotting what turned out to be their course to the All-Ireland final. It was a hungry Tyrone that defeated Derry by 2-6 to 1-7 at Omagh on 1 June. Derry got most of the possession. Even Tyrone admitted afterwards they were steeped. The Tyrone team that went on to threaten Kerry in the All-Ireland final could not get into the game at midfield. Yet they won. Dermot McNicholl was held scoreless, and the forwards were curtailed. When Damien Cassidy scored a Derry goal for the lead with six minutes to go, it only succeeded in provoking a Tyrone reply from Noel McGinn. Derry mourned that Plunkett Murphy and Damien Barton had won enough ball between them to win three championship matches.

When potential winners of the 1987 Ulster championship were being discussed, it was not Derry who were mentioned. Tyrone, Monaghan, Down were all tipped; Down were installed as favourites. Derry, the first team to meet them in the championship, duly obliged by knocking them out. Only two of Derry's forward line survived from the previous year: Enda Gormley and Dermot McNicholl. Gormley scored eight points, including the winner. Damien Cassidy sent a superb 23rd-minute left-footed shot crashing to the net. Derry won by 1-12 to 2-7.

The switch of Brian McGilligan to midfield from the centre-half-forward position where he spent the League campaign (he made a McKenna Cup appearance at full-forward) proved vital. Down's Liam Austin-Greg Blaney combination was well beaten. Dermot McNicholl was selected on the wing, lined out at centre-forward, and was clearly man of the match.

Derry needed a replay to beat Cavan in the semi-final. The first game was a day for robberies in Omagh. The armed variety made off with the gate receipts; both contestants got in on the act. After Dermot McNicholl's late goal transformed the game, Ronan Carolan stalled Derry with a last-minute equaliser for Cavan. The eighteen-year-old Dungiven lad Paul Kealy came on for his brother

Brian seventeen minutes into the replay and, just when the spectators were preparing for extra time, bagged a spectacular winning goal.

That was enough spectacle for one year. The Ulster final was unexciting—mainly because of the fact that Derry led 0-10 to 0-3 with twenty minutes remaining. Armagh were the opponents, 0-11 to 0-9 the final score, and Derry ran out of steam at half time to allow Armagh's fourteen men to come back into the game, inspired by Jim McKerr and Joe Kernan. Only when Joe Irwin ended a 21-minute scoring drought could Derry supporters breathe easily again, and Derry took the title by 0-11 to 0-9. "We made it difficult for ourselves," Dermot McNicholl commented. "In many ways they seemed to have the extra man."

McNicholl recalls: "We came through Ulster unexpectedly. We surprised ourselves. When we got to the semi-final stage we were really just looking forward to the occasion."

The All-Ireland semi-final was worse. McNicholl's heavily bandaged thigh indicated the folly of his playing at all. Derry froze. Meath meandered through their defence and won 0-15 to 0-8. Derry were too dependent on their big full-forward.

Meath scored two points within the first minute. It took Derry forty-eight minutes to score their first point from play. "It took us so long to settle down," said big Brian McGilligan, "I couldn't believe it, and yet we were only three points behind at half time. The injury to Dermot seemed to affect our motivation."

McNicholl said that he aggravated a hamstring injury in

the kick-out before the match. He tried it on the Friday before the game and it went. He just could not kick the ball with full power. It cost McNicholl and Derry the only goal chance of the game. That happened when Meath led 0-6 to 0-1 in the first half. If that had gone in, who knows? "The biggest disappointment about 1987", McNicholl recalls, "was that I didn't really get a chance."

Ulster champions have a knack of losing in the first round of the following year's campaign. The casualty list since Derry's resilience of the mid-1970s was truly astounding: Armagh in 1978 and 1983, Down in 1979 and 1982, Donegal in 1984, Tyrone in 1985, Monaghan in 1986, and now it was Derry's turn to join the injured. At Ballinascreen on 29 May 1988, Down ended the Derry reign by 1-11 to 0-7. Down led by just 0-4 to 0-2 at half time, but seemed to come to life when Dermot McNicholl was introduced as a Derry substitute. With eight minutes to go Mickey Lindon scored a goal for Down, and Derry's exit from the championship was asserted.

Derry's recovery in the National League was as spectacular as their descent. In 1985/86 they were brushing shoulders with Fermanagh, Sligo and Leitrim in the humility of Division 3 North. They qualified for a quarter-final that year, losing to Monaghan, and in two seasons they were back in the first division again, finishing third and fourth before the format was reorganised once more. In 1989 they qualified for a quarter-final in Croke Park, losing to Cavan before a paltry attendance of 6,213.

Derry went on a 4-15 to 1-7 romp against Fermanagh to

open the 1989 championship at Irvinestown. Enda Gormley from penalty, Damien Barton and Brian McGilligan with two beauties scored Derry's goals, but in Clones Derry laid the foundations for a new bogey when they succumbed to Donegal, 2-8 to 1-9. It might have been worse in the sweltering heat at Clones; Donegal shot seventeen wides, but Derry had a distinct advantage in Damien Barton, who was able to outfield the Donegal full-back John Connors. Again and again they exploited his height with balls dropping in to the goalmouth, and matters looked a lot better after twenty minutes (level) than they did after fifteen (when Derry trailed by 1-3 to 0-1). Enda Gormley got Derry's goal, Donegal recovered to lead 1-5 to 1-3 at half time, and after a Martin McHugh penalty in the forty-sixth minute Derry pressed the margin back to an elusive two points.

The Artane Boys' Band chose "The Town I Love So Well" for their musical programme on All-Ireland day. The alternatives included "They Call It Lovely Derry" and the rather more controversial "Derry Air". Collected in 1855 by the antiquarian George Petrie, it is best known today with the maudlin words of "Danny Boy", written as a nineteenth-century drawing-room ballad by Fred Weatherby, music by Jane Ross of Limavady, who copied it from a blind fiddler named McCurry. It is about a British soldier, as written by a father or a mother or a loved one, and, since the words have nothing to do either with city or county, Phil Coulter's haunting ballad about boyhood Derry was a much easier choice.

The odd thing about it is that Derry city is a GAA

wasteland. Just a couple of hundred spectators boarded the train for Croke Park on All-Ireland morning. A red-and-white flag fluttered in the breeze on Free Derry Corner. Soccer club Derry City changed the times of their League of Ireland matches to avoid clashing with the All-Ireland semi-final and final; but even when Derry City soccer club was in hibernation in the 1970s, the GAA in the city failed to revive. Derry city will be the first big test for the red-and-white rhapsody.

The impact of the win was to be seen in the Bogside, Creggan, Shantallow, and Waterside, and in the bunting over Shipquay Street and Unionhall Place. In the Bogside streets where Tommy Mellon and Big Tom McGuinness kept the games going there are dozens of flags on show. Someone has painted a big Sam on top of *You are now entering Free Derry*. Traffic in the city came to a halt when people took to the streets on Sunday evening. If the GAA in the county is to get a long-lasting benefit from their All-Ireland win, it will be in the city. It is easier for Gaelic to cross the sectarian divide in largely homogeneous Derry than in ghettoised Belfast. But even Derry city nationalists would have to be converted first.

Derry city must be one of the most culturally complex parts of Europe, all the product of war, of living with uninvited guests for 350 years, of being caught on the wrong side of a border it despised, and of its own sheer resourcefulness. The Siege of Derry celebrations in 1989 were an extraordinary sight to behold. It was the Teagues who did the celebrating, and the loyalists mourned that their party had been hijacked. Now the All-Ireland had been won, was this the chance for the Prods' revenge? Journalist Éamonn McCann sparked off a debate on a BBC radio programme when he claimed that unionists resented the Derry victory simply because Catholics were having a good time, and added that, in general, Fenians have more fun.

Local GAA official Charlie Bonner was in Dublin in 1974. He remembers it took so long to get Tallaght and Blanchardstown into football togs, but how much Kevin Heffernan's victory helped. Now he detects the same thing in Derry. "Gaelic has been growing in the city since Celtic Park was done up and reopened." Eleven primary schools now field teams, but pitches and personnel remain a problem, and the best that a city of 74,000 can field is a second-division team in the county league. But Derry is cosmopolitan, and has probably seen more fads come and go than even the four Irish cities that are larger than it. Yesterday the Undertones, today this fifteen-a-side handling game, tomorrow bungee-jumping. Perhaps it was through the haze of a week of celebration, but as Sam arrived in the Guildhall on the Friday after the All-Ireland, for the first time since footballers wore knickerbockers and Waterside hurlers went to an All-Ireland semi-final, it looked just about possible.

At the last count, there have been eleven attempts to revive GAA in soccer-obsessed Derry city. The yellowing pages of the *Derry Journal* are full of references to them, most notably those when soccer was affected by world war in 1913 and 1943. The latest came in 1990 with the clearing of rubbish off Celtic Park, within a poc fada's length of Derry City's Brandywell, and its reopening as an inter-county venue.

"Derry city is our North Sea oil," a county official told a 1980s convention. Derry GAA realise they have vast potential resources there to sustain future success, but the drilling rights don't come cheap. For since the 1880s Derry's clergy and nationalist community chose soccer as their sport, expressing their identity in the eleven-a-side game that is played on a day that the bishop approved.

The city clubs with beautiful names—Emeralds and Sunburst, the esteemed St Patrick's from Waterside that won the intricately carved 1891 hurling cup, or the Éire Óg team who provided Derry's first inter-provincial player—all are no more. Now just one intermediate and three junior clubs serve the city. The street teams of the 1930s and 1940s failed to follow the population to the new suburbs of the 1950s, and there are neither pitches nor personnel to revive the game there now.

The question of how the GAA collapsed so completely in Derry city has never properly been resolved. "The ban did not help," Roddy Gribben recalls. "But the bishop of Derry at that time, Neil Farren, was anti-Gaelic. The college did not play Gaelic when he was president." Derry city was not the only area hit by the ban. St Martin's of Desertmartin had to pull out of the 1935 county league pending the appeal of some of their players against suspension under the foreign games rule. Ballinascreen lost so many players under the rule in 1936 that they had to call on players from Desertmartin and surrounding areas.

But a 1943 boom in Gaelic games seemed to have reversed that trend. In October of that year the GAA purchased a ground formerly used by soccer clubs, Celtic

Park. Soon there were seventeen teams in the city, as new clubs seemed to spring up on every street of the Bogside, augmenting the existing Seán Dolans, Éire Óg, Robert Emmets, John Mitchels and St Columb's clubs. St Patrick's, Pearses, James Connollys, Sarsfields, Seán Larkins, Wolfe Tones and Kevin Barrys among others spent Sundays in competition in the new field. Many of them did not survive the winter, but the enthusiasm meant that the debt on the field was paid off in seven weeks.

The collapse of this new enthusiasm coincided with the construction of Derry's suburbs in the 1950s. As people moved out to the Creggan, the teams, based on the closely knit street communities, failed to move with them. Re-establishing clubs in the suburbs proved too great a drain on GAA personnel. Éire Óg won the city's last county championship in 1952. Only Seán Dolans and clubs such as Doire Cholm Cille kept going, and with the advent of the troubles GAA activity almost ceased altogether in the city.

Soccer teams coped better with the relocation. Now there are twenty-five junior soccer clubs in the city, with over a thousand players affiliated to the Derry and District Football Association, an organisation affiliated to neither the IFA nor FAI.

In 1990 Derry GAA tried again, and have spent £400,000 developing Celtic Park. But the suburbs remain the key to the GAA's problems the city.

Derry, with 62,697 inhabitants, is the fifth-largest of Ireland's seven cities. Coleraine, with a population of 15,967, Limavady with 8,014 and Portstewart with 5,312 could hardly muster a decent team between them to compete in the Derry club championship. Seán O'Connell, top scorer on

Gaelic teams for twenty years, now lives in Limavady. The area divides equally between unionists and nationalists, and its council recently passed to nationalist hands for the first time in its history, yet there is only one good GAA club. In Coleraine and the north-east, where there is a growing nationalist minority, there is also one club.

By choosing the first round of the 1990 championship clash with Fermanagh to reopen Celtic Park, Derry were at least reasonably confident of starting the eleventh revival of Gaelic games in the city on a winning note. Damien Cassidy was the revelation of the game, scoring two goals and having a third shot rebound off the post for Fergal McCusker to finish the ball to the net. Derry won by 4-14 to 0-7 and faced Donegal again in a semi-final tie that clashed with the performance of one of Donegal's favourite sons, Packie Bonner, in Ireland's World Cup tie against Egypt.

It was Declan Bonner (no relation) who delighted Donegal men and sent Derry into depression. But the talking point for Derry that evening was Damien Barton's penalty. He was seriously barracked as he approached the kick and sent it harmlessly wide. It came early in the game, but was enough to indicate that this was not going to be Derry's day. Manus Boyle got a Donegal goal after fourteen minutes, and Derry went harmlessly out of the championship, 1-15 to 0-8. Losing to Donegal was becoming a habit.

8

BACK TO THE FUTURE
1991–1993

In November 1990 Éamonn Coleman was appointed Derry team manager. They wanted a winning team, and they were prepared to let the team drop back into Division 3 if it was necessary.

Coleman came with a reputation. A non-drinker, a bricklayer, he had been a tough forward on Derry teams between 1966 and 1973, and was suspended for twelve months on two separate occasions. Admittedly his two suspensions had been for technicalities. Never once was he sent off. In the late seventies he was found to have played for three teams in the one year, and in 1985, at the end of the All-Ireland under-21 final in which Cork beat Derry, he was considered to have been moving forcibly in the direction of the referee when one of his players intercepted him. To this day, Coleman insists that the referee, Carthage Buckley, was a friend of his and he was only going to talk to him about a particular decision.

"Éamonn Coleman took over when Derry was at an all-time low, and he restored pride in the team," team captain Henry Downey says. "Everyone was talking about the talent that Derry had produced at under-age level and in the colleges, but it was a matter of developing that into a senior team capable of winning titles. Éamonn realised he had players in the county. He knew the players from minor

and under-21 and also from Jordanstown. They had respect
for him. Attitudes had to change, and he brought in a more
disciplined regime. Mickey Moran also played a big part,
because he is a great trainer."

"No-one will ever understand how with all the good
minor and under-21 teams we had we could never make
the breakthrough at senior level," Damien Cassidy says.
"The answer was simple. We were never organised.
Certainly not the way we are now. After winning the minor
All-Ireland we had two strong under-21 teams in 1985 and
1986; that gave us thirty players along with the senior
players at the time, and if we had organised properly we
would have sustained a serious challenge for the championship. It was an ideal time: it was the end of the Kerry
era, and Meath were the team coming through the ranks
who should have been making an impression. It didn't
happen. We went from year to year without any direction.
We lost players with great talent, like Declan McNicholl
and Eddie McElhinney, because there was no real
organisation. Each summer came round and we won one
game or two and then the championship was over. That all
changed when Éamonn Coleman came round. He had
coached minor and under-21 teams, and he changed
everything, and he brought the right men in with him. He
had personality, drive, desire; he knew he had players with
ability. He insisted on a full commitment. Training became
organised. It was the right kind of training. The players
began to realise that something could be achieved."

The call to return and manage Derry came at an important

time in Éamonn Coleman's life. In 1985 Éamonn and his wife had separated; he left for London a few months later. "I had no ambition to come back home for anything else," he honestly explains. "I was travelling back to see the children every month or so anyway, but I went to London to get myself going again, to do something, and I enjoyed my life there. It's different coming home to live with your aunt and your father [his father died last November] and not coming home to live with your wife, but you have to get over these things. And football makes up for an awful lot of things in life.

"In the last few years Gary and myself have a better relationship now than ever before. The first year I was picking on him on the field, but I've caught myself on now. He's a shy character and he's a great footballer."

Another son, Vivian, played on the 1993 Derry minor team. "He's a bad boy on the field. He's a rough character all right. He plays football like I did, you know. Gary is not like that at all. Now Margaret, my daughter—she's now twenty-two—she was a better footballer than either of the boys. She played centre-three-quarters on the under-12 team in the boys' schools final. She got her hair cropped specially, and the way she carried a ball she'd go through you if you weren't careful. She was so dirty she would have killed her brothers on the field."

The advent of a second young minor team with a winning tradition was also to change attitudes in the squad. "All the young boys have won minor All-Irelands," Brian McGilligan says. "The older lads might have had doubts before, because they have been about for a long time and putting in an effort with no reward."

If Derry's All-Ireland minor success of 1965 was closely connected with that of St Colum's in the colleges championship, that of 1989 was allied to the success of St Patrick's, Maghera. Winners of seven Ulster titles in thirteen years and twice-beaten All-Ireland finalists, St Patrick's had the look of a team that was going to go all the way in 1989.

As a result, Derry had to play the first round of the 1989 Ulster minor championship with eight county players and seven Maghera players who barely knew each other—who had only met at one training session. Having identified eight key players on the Maghera college team that they wanted to join the county panel, Derry's selectors waited for the news that the Maghera players' commitment to their college had ended. Maghera played some magnificent football in the colleges championship, and all who were there still talk about the great clash with St Colman's from Newry, which Maghera won by 4-10 to 1-9. Meanwhile Derry lost all but one of their matches in the Ulster minor league, earning just one draw for consolation. Monaghan won the League.

Then, just as St Colum's had in 1965, Maghera won the All-Ireland. The introductions were completed, and Derry set to their task. They beat Fermanagh by five points, and by the second round of the championship the Maghera boys had got to know their colleagues. The tie with Cavan was one of the best matches Derry followers can remember in any grade.

Derry trailed by five points at half time, Cavan scored

another goal soon afterwards, and Derry heads were dropping when they brought on Maghera player Eunan O'Kane, moved him on to the right wing to link up with his clubmate Ryan Murphy, banking on the fact that the two players would know each other's game and work well together. It worked a dream: O'Kane set Murphy up for a goal then scored 2-2 himself. Cavan scored another goal near the end, and with Derry needing a point to draw, O'Kane audaciously weaved through to score a goal from twenty-one yards.

Derry were unstoppable after that. They beat Armagh and New York at Ballinascreen, and sank Roscommon by eighteen points with a devastating second-half performance in the All-Ireland semi-final, 4-16 to 1-7. They stayed at the International Airport Hotel and went back there for the All-Ireland final. The father of one of the players booked up Stillorgan bowling alley on the night before the game, so the team worked out their All-Ireland butterflies with a good game of bowling.

Winning by 3-9 to 1-6 in the All-Ireland final might have been enough. Derry did it the hard way. They missed a penalty and several other goal opportunities. They also had nine wides, to five for Offaly.

Derry team manager John Joe Kearney had watched Offaly against Kerry. He worked out that Offaly's strength was their midfield. "They seemed to build a lot around their midfield. Our midfielders were told they had to win a lot of possession or to stop other fellows getting a good supply." And towering midfielder Anthony Tohill captured the spirit of the new Derry. His high fielding, strong running and prodigious right boot (two of his three points came from forty-fives) augured well for the future.

Declan Bateson scored the first goal from an acute angle in the eighteenth minute. Offaly conceded 23rd and 24th-minute penalties for fouls on James Lynn and Bateson. Éamonn Burns converted the first, but the second was deflected onto the bar at full stretch by Offaly goalkeeper and captain Daragh Scully, one of the best saves in Croke Park for a long time. Bateson set up Dermot Heaney for the killer goal after forty-nine minutes following a long ball by Gary Coleman. Offaly team manager Christy Hand was magnanimous in defeat, telling the Derry men, "I sincerely hope that you will go all the way and win Sam."

This was a team from the GAA heartlands as never before. The only Derry city player on the team, Dolan O'Hagan, was sidelined with a broken collar-bone for most of the championship. Some four thousand people welcomed home the Tom Markham Cup. Gerry Thornley wrote in the *Irish Times*: "Derry folk can be forgiven for feeling a mite smug about the future for they have the best crop of under-18 footballers in the country at the moment. That much was confirmed in emphatic style at Croke Park in this unexpectedly comprehensive defeat of Offaly in the All-Ireland minor final."

The 1989 minor team was: Martin O'Connor, J. Martin, F. McAllister, G. Simpson, B. McGonigle, Gary Coleman, R. Skelly, J. Mulholland, Anthony Tohill, Rory McEldowney, James Lynn, Éamonn Burns, Eunan O'Kane, Dermot Heaney, Declan Bateson. Substitutes: K. Diamond for Martin, R. Murphy for Lynn.

Maghera repeated the success in 1990, a disappointing final against St Jarlath's, Tuam, leading *Irish Times* sports writer Pat Roche to plead that he hoped that the boys were better at getting points in the Leaving Cert than they were on the football field; but after just three minutes of the replay Dermot Dougan had the ball in the net, and Maghera held out for a narrow-squeak 1-11 to 0-13 victory. Geoffrey McGonigle kicked five points in that game.

Derry minors went on to repeat their 1989 colleagues' Ulster success with a fascinating 2-10 to 2-8 victory over Down. The highlight of the Ulster final was Derry's early goal, a superb fifty-metre run from midfield finished to the net by Ollie Collins. Hugh Mullan got a second before half time, and then forty seconds of madness saw Down take back two goals, and Derry had to come from behind to win by two points.

The 1990 Maghera team was: J. Murtagh, K. Bateson, R. McCloskey, G. Simpson, M. McGonigle, B. McGonigle, K. Diamond, B. McCormack, H. Mullan, E. O'Kane, D. Dougan, E. Burns, G. McGonigle, R. Murphy, P. McGuigan. Substitute: K. Ryan for McGuigan.

The 1990 Derry minor team was: D. Hasson, K. Diamond, B. McCosker, G. Simpson, B. McGonigle, J. Mulholland, H. Mullan, E. O'Kane, O. Collins, D. Dougan, R. Murphy, E. Burns, G. McGonigle. Substitute: B. McCormack for Burns.

If there is a negative side to the Derry success story it is how the progress of hurling was brought to a resounding halt. By early 1991 half of the hurling team were dual players, and a real breakthrough in the game that was partially descended from that of old-time Burt and the Dungiven ballad seemed likely. Now the tenders of the cammons tradition have to find a new set of representatives for their county.

The memory of the Derry hurlers of the first decade of the twentieth century had long since passed away. Hurling activity had resumed as early as 1930 with a little help from just across the newly established Donegal border. Burt won two consecutive Derry championships and helped Derry reach the Ulster senior final (then ranked junior for All-Ireland purposes) for the last time in 1931. The match was played at Belfast on 5 July, and Derry were severely crushed by Antrim, by 4-10 to 0-1. Antrim defeated Galway before they were beaten by Waterford in the All-Ireland final. Burt hurlers appeared with Derry when they were eliminated by Donegal in the 1932 Ulster hurling semi-final.

But the old hurling strongholds in the city and Inishowen were in decline. Sarsfields won the 1933 and 1934 titles before the hurling championship eventually passed from the city area in 1935, when the Shamrocks from Lavey won. Derry city's last title came in 1937, when the Aileach club won back the title. The mantle passed to Ballinascreen St Colm's in 1938 and 1939, Lavey in 1940, 1941, and 1944, John Mitchels of Coleraine in 1945, Lavey in 1946, and Coleraine in 1947, until Lavey and St Finbarr's took command of the title for nineteen years. Slaughtneil won three in a row in 1966–68, and Dungiven dominated the championship in the 1960s and 1970s.

Derry fielded a team in the Ulster junior championship annually but were easy prey to Antrim, Down, and even Armagh and Donegal. When Liam Hinphy arrived from

County Kilkenny in 1963, Derry had four adult clubs in the county, there was no juvenile activity, and little attention was paid to the game at county board level. Alf Murray's presidency of the GAA saw the initiation of a five-year plan, designed to ensure that every county had a minor team in action by 1969. Subsidised hurleys were made available and an under-14 competition initiated. The catchment areas of local secondary schools were used to establish new hurling clubs in Derry. Competitions were established at under-12, under-14 and minor level.

Eight teams entered those 1960s competitions, and coaches were sent to Gormanston to improve the teaching of the game. The Dungiven under-14s won their section in Féile na nGael, defeating Ardeen from Louth by 7-4 to nil in Thurles in 1971 and Portaferry of Down by 1-5 to 1-2 in Waterford in 1977, winning in Kilkenny and in Division B of their section in Croke Park in 1982. Building on Dungiven's Féile na nGael teams, Derry won new hurling honours in competitions specially designed for weaker counties, in under-21 hurling in 1970, minor and under-16 in 1972, minor in 1974, junior in 1975, and under-16 again in 1984. Derry senior hurlers played superbly in the B All-Ireland championships in 1979 and 1982. In 1986 their under-21 hurlers went to Loughgiel and beat Antrim by an amazing 3-21 to 1-6, the first competitive win over Antrim in any grade of hurling for eighty years. The following year the under-21s beat Antrim again, only to lose to Down in the All-Ireland semi-final.

These achievements were matched by the successes of the minor teams of 1990 and 1991, who won Ulster titles and put in fine performances against Cork and Kilkenny in the All-Ireland semi-finals. St Patrick's College in Maghera and St Patrick's High School in Dungiven won Ulster championships, and Maghera put up a superb performance against St Colman's of Fermoy in the All-Ireland colleges semi-final.

Fifteen minutes into that 1990 All-Ireland minor hurling semi-final, Derry and mighty Cork were level, 1-5 each. At half time it was 1-7 to 1-5, and with Cork down to fourteen men it looked as if Derry were on course for the biggest upset in under-18 hurling since Meath reached the All-Ireland final of sixty-one years earlier. In the end, points from Cork's Damien Fleming saved the Munster champions and put Derry out by 1-14 to 1-9. A year later Derry beat Down by 4-14 to 1-7 and Antrim by a two-point margin of 3-10 to 2-11 in the Ulster final and held Kilkenny to three points in the All-Ireland semi-final, going down by 0-15 to 2-6.

The 1990 Derry minor hurling team: Fergal McNally, G. Simpson, H. Mullan, J. Young, R. Stevenson, P. McCloy, P. Cartin, D. Murray, M. McCloskey, M. McKenna, O. Collins, B. McCormack, Michael Collins, P. McEldowney, G. McGonigle. Substitute: S. Downey for McGonigle.

Derry won the 1992 Ulster under-21 championships with players who were used to winning, players like Geoffrey McGonigle, already an All-Ireland colleges football and Ulster colleges hurling medallist, an Ulster minor and under-21 medallist in both codes, and county senior medallist in both codes with Dungiven. Fergal McNally was goalkeeper on that team.

Strangely enough, the primary school is in Derry city, ancient stronghold of the game, while only three primary schools play the game in rural Derry.

After finishing third-last in Division 3 in 1984/85, the performances of Derry seniors, too, began to improve in the National Hurling League. In 1986/87 Derry narrowly missed promotion after finishing level on points with Roscommon and Carlow. In 1987/88 they were promoted, losing only to Meath and beating former Leinster semi-finalists Kildare to second place. The 1988/89 campaign saw Derry senior hurling's finest winter. Placed in the same division as Clare, Cork, Dublin, and Laois, they managed three points, but their most astounding performance was 1-11 to 1-9, a defeat against Cork in Lavey.

Derry were leading by four points with ten minutes to go. Cork got a free, which came back off the post; if it had gone over the bar, Derry would have caused the greatest shock in the history of hurling. It was a wet day, on a tight pitch, and Cork had four early points before Derry got a chance to play a bit. A relieved Cork coach, Joe McGrath, commented afterwards that the team could have gone home but the selectors could not. Henry Downey, Séamus Downey, Tony Scullion, Brian McGilligan, John McGurk, Ciarán McGurk and Colm McGurk were all on that hurling team. Séamus Downey also scored 1-2 for Ulster in the Railway Shield final of 1992, but most of the dual players were forced to opt out of hurling because of football commitments.

Derry co-operated with the Ulster Council's ambitious relaunch of the Ulster senior hurling championship in

1989. In 1990 they were heavily beaten by Down in Armagh, 1-23 to 1-5, their goal coming from Brian McGilligan in the dying minutes. Derry hurlers faced a problem with dual stars: eight of their team are also senior footballers, and in 1991 their understrength team suffered an even heavier defeat, 6-13 to 2-10, despite trailing by only 2-8 to 1-8 at half time. It was a portent of things to come. In 1992 Derry were beaten by 9-18 to 0-10, one of the heaviest defeats in the long history of hurling in the county and eight points heavier than the ignominy suffered against Dublin in that long-grass All-Ireland semi-final of eighty-eight years before.

Derry reverted to the senior B championship in 1993, despite Gregory Biggs's achievement in scoring 2-9 against Monaghan, a record for the entire 1993 hurling championship. Derry went out in the semi-final by 0-18 to 2-8 against the eventual winners, Meath. More disappointing was the defeat of the minors by 6-18 to 1-8 against Down.

One common advantage all Ulster's teams have enjoyed in the 1990s has been the benefit of a high profile. Since the BBC's sports department turned its attention to Ulster's championship four years ago, an entire new audience has been found for the games. The BBC were attracted to Gaelic because it offered a summer game, often played in sunshine, with large, colourful crowds as a backdrop. It also offered lots of scores and a healthy sprinkling of incident. The Ulster final became the biggest operation in the calendar of the BBC's sports department. It was all a far cry from 1934, when the BBC decided not to carry GAA sports results because it would cause offence to the majority of their radio listeners.

"BBC's championship programme has made football here," says Danny Quinn. "When I started teaching four years ago, when you went into a classroom it was Manchester United jerseys and Liverpool jerseys. Now you go into a classroom and, depending on which is the Gaelic team doing well at the time, it is all Down jerseys or Donegal jerseys, Tyrone jerseys—everything; and it is all Derry jerseys at the minute. Everybody is watching it—both sides of the community."

"They all watch the game on television," says Joe Brolly, who is meeting with compliments on his performance against Dublin from all manner of unexpected sources on the Northern Circuit, where he practises as a barrister. "It's a big step up in the ladder excitement-wise from soccer or any other sport."

In Éamonn Coleman's first match of the 1991 championship against Monaghan, ten thousand spectators watched Enda Gormley's return to the team. The victory was by an impressive five points, but Derry were discomfited by the fact that seven of their points came from frees and a further two from wing-back John McGurk, spiritually renewed by Lavey's All-Ireland club victory and already making a reputation for winging his way onto scoresheets. Éamonn Coleman declared: "We have the best footballers in the province, and we aim to prove it by winning the All-Ireland. But we have a lot to do."

Considering that no Ulster team had won an All-Ireland

since 1968, it was high-minded talk, but instead of Derry it was their semi-final opponents, Down, who went on to win the All-Ireland. Derry got out of jail the first day; having fallen 0-11 to 0-4 behind, they brought on Joe Brolly and he inspired a revival. Within sixty seconds of his arrival, taking the place of Colm McGurk at corner-forward, Brolly had set up Derry's second point from play from the ill-fated Dermot McNicholl. Down promptly took off his marker, Brendan McKernan, because he was not rising to the task of matching Brolly, and the referee was expressing undue interest in the legality of some of his tackles in the meantime.

Brian McGilligan made a great catch at midfield, played a neat one-two with McNicholl, soloed goalwards and sent to Éamonn Burns, who scrambled the ball into the net. It finished 1-10 to 0-13. Phew, and back to the athletic grounds for the replay.

The spectators had to contend with a free every eighty seconds, nine books (four for Derry men), and Greg Blayney and Fergal McCusker sent off within two minutes of each other in the second half by referee Michael Greenan. Their hopes for a better game the second time round were not realised. A bewildering series of switches backfired, man of the match Ross Carr scored nine points for Down, and Derry bowed out by 0-14 to 0-9. "They puzzled themselves more than they did us," Mickey Linden declared.

Five wins in a row made it a superb 1991/92 in the reorganised National League for Derry, beating Down,

Kerry, Kildare, Meath, and Offaly. Nevertheless, the National League semi-final double bill of Meath v. Derry and Dublin v. Tyrone brought a crowd of 30,594 to Croke Park. Dublin and Meath had played their four-times thriller the previous summer, shattering all attendance records for matches at the provincial stages of the championships. Somehow, in one of those turnabout days that sport trumps up with refreshing frequency, neither made it to the All-Ireland final. Derry won by 0-12 to 1-8, Enda Gormley scoring four points and Anthony Tohill three. It ensured an all-Ulster National League final for the first time since 1983 and the third time in history. It also gave Derry the opening to take the National Football League for the second time.

Winning teams normally need luck, but not usually in the helpings required when Derry beat Tyrone by 1-10 to 1-8 in the 1992 National League final. To say that Derry's success was greeted with exasperation is putting it mildly. Paddy Downey wrote in the *Irish Times*: "Tyrone were the better football team, more skilful and composed, more cohesive and constructive, until it came to the vital matter of scoring, and that, scoring, was what counted at the end of the day. Derry, who trailed their rivals over the greater part of the game, were in front at the full time whistle and thus it can be argued deserved their victory." Downey accorded "to Derry the spoils and to Tyrone a good deal more than a half share of the glory which is poor consolation for losers in any sport."

Only fools and dreamers thought Derry might win this match as they absorbed continuous Tyrone pressure in the closing quarter. Damian McCusker saved a Tyrone point, leaping high enough to punch the ball back out, another Tyrone point was inexplicably disallowed by referee Tommy Howard, later to take charge of the 1993 All-Ireland, and Tyrone wasted enough chances to ensure that there were only three points in the difference with two minutes of normal time remaining.

Then came the sucker punch. Declan Bateson almost snatched a goal from nothing, and Anthony Tohill landed the resulting fifty into the goalmouth. Tyrone's match star Plunkett Donaghy and goalkeeper Finbarr McConnell both put up their hands, but neither collected, and the ball bounced up into the net. Tohill added a point, Noel Donnelly missed one for Tyrone, and Dermot Heaney gave Derry their victory with a point in the second minute of injury time.

In fact Derry had risen to their task during stages of the game, after trailing 0-4 to nil after a slow first quarter. Derry brought it back level, at 0-5 each, Tyrone led by 0-6 to 0-5 at half time, and Derry had in fact taken a 0-8 to 0-7 lead before Tyrone's goal from the previous year's under-21 star, Peter Canavan, in the forty-fifth minute. Derry were only denied a goal by a brilliant Finbarr McConnell save, one of the best of all time in a League final, just before Tohill's freak fifty. But as far as the reaction from the media was concerned, this was a smash-and-grab title, and Derry were the bandits.

Coleman commented: "We were disgusted with what people wrote about how we stole the game and how we did this and did that. We put the ball in the net to draw level, and then we went and won the match. If Tyrone could not score that wasn't our fault. The papers slated us."

The Derry team was: Damien McCusker; Kieran McKeever, Danny Quinn, Tony Scullion; Henry Downey (captain), Colm Rafferty, Gary Coleman; Brian McGilligan, Dermot Heaney 0-1; Anthony Tohill 1-5, Dermot McNicholl, Gary McGill 0-1; Joe Brolly 0-1, Fergal McCusker 0-1, Enda Gormley 0-1. Substitutes: Séamus Downey for McNicholl, John McGurk for Rafferty, Declan Bateson for McGill.

As luck would have it, Derry and Tyrone were pitted against each other just a fortnight later in the first round of the championship. This was to mark a return of championship football to Derry city at the revamped Celtic Park. For safety reasons the crowd was to be limited to ten thousand (although twelve thousand squeezed in), and in compensation BBC television stepped in to cover the match live for the first time since the 1966 Ulster final was carried live from Casement Park. Derry made two changes from the League final, Tyrone one, and those who knew Ulster football predicted a tense and untidy game in the narrow confines of the Derry city venue. The total of sixty-one frees proved them right. Four players from each side were booked in the first twenty one minutes.

This time Derry won 1-10 to 1-7. At midfield Dermot Heaney and Brian McGilligan overwhelmed Plunkett Donaghy and Ciarán Corr, and Derry established control of the game by the fifth minute, when Tohill and Séamus Downey sent Dermot Heaney through for a crashing fourteen-yard goal. Gary Coleman helped Tyrone back into it with an own goal, and the sides were level at half time, but three Derry points in the first three minutes of the second half set the scene for the rest of the game, and Derry led by five points with three minutes to go.

"We proved our point in the championship," as Éamonn Coleman said so proudly at the end of this game. Danny Quinn concurred: "We were far better the second time round. We were sharper and hungrier and we did very well at midfield. Our corner-backs held their men perfectly, and we gave a far better display than we did two weeks ago. In the second half they never really threatened us." Dermot McNicholl commented: "Our pride was hurt when we got so little credit for winning the league. Against Tyrone the second time the stakes were raised physically, and we came through. Brian McGilligan had a great game and as a result put more pressure on the Tyrone defence. It was a tough afternoon."

According to McGilligan, "we were very determined to get clean possession. They broke the ball down a lot during the League final, but in the championship, on a tight pitch, we kept the supply going." John Donnelly, Tyrone manager, said: "We tried to mix it with a bigger team, which was probably a mistake. On a small pitch like that we were getting it hard on every fifty-fifty ball. We never took control of the game."

Against Monaghan, Derry led by 0-10 to 0-1 at half time but were rattled by one of those legendary comebacks that are a feature of Ulster football. Goals from Stephen McGinnity, Ray McCarron and Kevin Hughes gave

Monaghan a two-point lead. Declan Bateson got a Derry goal, and when in the dying seconds Gerry Moen got an equalising point for Monaghan there was no time for the kick-out to be taken.

It was back to Celtic Park for the replay, and this time Derry won by 2-9 to 0-7 in a game marred by forty first-half frees. Gary Coleman, from a 22nd-minute penalty, and Declan Bateson got the Derry goals. Asked by a journalist if he was pleased, Éamonn Coleman replied, "We won."

There are many questions for Derry to answer, commented Liam Stirrat, Monaghan manager. They did not manage their first score from play until almost half an hour, and could score only five second-half points despite their dominance.

In disposing of the All-Ireland champions, Down, by 0-15 to 0-12, seven Derry players and ten in all were booked, and eventually Down's Peter Withnell was sent off. The match attracted a thirty thousand crowd, and they saw an exciting tie. "Our tackling and commitment were big factors in our win," said Coleman. Derry came back to equalise three times in the first half, held a four-point lead with fifteen minutes to go, saw it brought back to one point, then went ahead with two points from Gormley and another from Cassidy. "That was a great occasion for us," Enda Gormley says. "It was possibly not the best game I played but certainly the most satisfying. We just went with a single purpose that day, to win. I just think that if we had been playing till now we wouldn't get beaten."

Derry had now gone eighteen matches without defeat and eliminated the reigning All-Ireland champions. They faced one hoodoo still, the Donegal factor. The Ulster final was always going to be a rugged affair: Donegal's John Cunningham was sent off for a second bookable offence, and Gary Coleman, playing as the spare man in the second half for Derry, proved too inexperienced for the task. Losing Tohill through injury proved too great a handicap for Derry. They were level with the wind in the second half, but when Damien Barton scored a point it was the signal for three great Donegal scores. Séamus Downey's goal after fifty minutes gave Derry the lead, despite a suspicion of more than one player in the square, and Donegal came back to win. Declan Bonner scored the equaliser, Murray scored two points, and Donegal won by 0-14 to 1-9.

Great was the disappointment. A wily Donegal team outwitted them, Tom Humphries wrote in the *Irish Times*. "This should have been Derry's day; it wasn't. The National League champions failed to consummate the promise of spring and early summer. At the end, by which time they might have just snatched an undeserved draw, they were playing with some coherence but no commitment."

"We knew we could have gone all the way," says Anthony Tohill. "And then it all went wrong." Tohill watched the second half from the sideline, having broken two bones in his foot.

"Losing in the Ulster final in 1992 totally changed the Derry team," team captain Henry Downey says. "We had a lot of confidence before that Ulster final after beating Down. It was confidence which was based on one game: it wasn't based on the fact that Derry had produced performances over a period of time."

Éamonn Coleman recalls: "It took me two or three months to get my appetite back for football after that defeat. We didn't perform against Donegal. We had built up our whole campaign to play Down. When we beat them we patted ourselves on the back and forgot about Donegal and got caught. In the end I decided to stay on only because the team was so young." When he saw the draw for the 1993 championship—Down in the first round—Coleman says he was sorry he didn't take the boat.

Derry brush off the charges that they are a dirty team. No player was sent off in the 1993 championship, and even the grudge match with Donegal escaped without major incident. Derry officials point to their internal disciplinary record. Ballinderry were once suspended for two years because of a free-for-all, and when the 1982 county championship final between Ballinderry and Dungiven erupted into a fist-fight the entire championship was declared null and void and no medals awarded. "Maybe I'm looking at Derry through false glasses," Éamonn Coleman says, "but I don't see the team as a dirty team. They're a physical, strong team, but they're also disciplined. When we went to Newry for the first round of the 1993 championship, as far as I was concerned it was Down who dished it out. They had half a dozen men booked, one sent off, and two more were lucky not to go.

"I was a tough player myself, and a very physical player for my size, but I never got the line in my life. I was very fast, and I was skilful with the ball, and I could look after myself with my elbows. Elbows are great things. They keep people off, especially the bigger fellows. I developed a certain use for my elbows, especially in club games, where you needed all the protection you could get. But I didn't think I was considered dirty. One thing I had was a great side-step. If you were running at me, for instance, and you wanted to hit me and I had the ball, I'd go by you and leave you dead. That's what I was best at doing as a player.

"I think Gaelic football is a man's game. There's no pussy-footing about it. If you're not a man you shouldn't be out there. That aspect is very important to me, but it's not all that I like about the game. You have to be clever and be an excellent athlete to play Gaelic football well. Most people may not believe me when I say that's what's most important, but that's what I believe in."

In the circumstances, the Battle of Lavey in February 1993 came at an embarrassing time for Derry GAA, when the bitterness of coverage of Derry GAA affairs, notably the Battle of Ballinascreen in 1968 and the Battle of Croke Park in 1973, had long receded. This should really have been Lavey's tour de force after their heroics of 1991: a home match against O'Donovan Rossa in the All-Ireland club championship. Instead it all whirlpooled away in twelve minutes of chaos, after which the team captains were brought together and told by referee Séamus Prior that he was going to abandon the match unless the dornálaíocht came to an end.

Damien Doherty was booked before a ball was kicked. Séamus Downey and John O'Donovan were booked for a little sparring. Ciarán McGurk was sent off for dumping an opponent off the ball. Hugh Martin McGurk was also sent off when Pat Davis was found sprawling on the ground away from the ball in another incident. And his departure caused another free-for-all before Prior took the captains to task for the clandestine warfare. He had only two more bookings to make before half time and none thereafter, but he got a puck for himself at half time from an irate Lavey supporter, and the whole matter of staging major semi-finals in the home venues of clubs was called into question.

Lavey were two men down at that stage and, although they trailed by three points at half time, were showing some of the ball-contending spirit that has inspired teams that were one or two men down before: teams like Dublin's All-Ireland winning Dirty Dozen on the same day as Johnny McGurk collected his minor medal in 1983. Dublin's win that day was helped by a goalkeeper's miskick, and the same thing happened in Lavey in 1993, only in reverse. Brendan Regan's kick-out fell to Don Davis, and he hand-passed the ball over a Lavey defender for Mick McCarthy to score. McCarthy sent to John Brady for a second soon afterwards. Lavey lost by 2-10 to 0-4 and formed a saffron guard of honour to applaud their opponents off the field.

It was almost polite, but the shouting was not over yet. When the press doled out blame afterwards, Lavey were the ones who got most of it. Tom O'Riordan, writing in the *Irish Independent,* said he had never been as frightened that someone would be injured as he had been in Ballinascreen that day, and Lavey resentment lived on through the summer until the success of the county team helped put things right.

"We made mistakes on the day and we were more than punished for them," Johnny McGurk recalls. "The press we got was terrible after the way that Lavey had performed for the two or three years before that. As far as club football was concerned it was a one-off. Certainly I wouldn't condone everything that went on that day, but I felt we were made an example of in the press. We did not approach that match any differently from the way we approached any other game. Lavey are not a physical side. They have always been hard and always been fair, and I think everybody would agree to that before the match. We didn't approach the game any differently. We had exactly the same preparation as before. Perhaps our downfall was that we watched Skibbereen too much. We had too many videos of them. And we had probably given them too much respect. We watched them too much and knew too much about them … We lost our discipline early, and once we lost one man we were onto a losing battle from that. You only have a few chances to get to an All-Ireland club championship, and perhaps the occasion does get the better of you, but we did some very stupid things that day."

After Derry beat Louth by 1-11 to 0-10 in the final round of the 1992/93 League, Desmond Fahy wrote: "This can be a very simple game. Derry, by no means the most florid or ornamental of performers, have been the dominant team in the League for the past two years because they are strong in the central positions. From full back through to full forward, the spine is solid. When these central six players function as a coherent unit, they are a formidable prospect."

Donegal's defeat of Derry in the 1993 National League quarter-final was the toughest encounter between the teams to date. Seán Kilfeather reported in the *Irish Times*: "Recrimination, bitterness and injury were piled on each other at the end of this National Football League match when Donegal came from behind to edge their way into the semi-finals. The match was far from being a violent one but there was an atmosphere of ill will from the start and the referee, Brian White from Wexford, did not seem to have the desired effect as he tried to sort out what appeared to be a number of personal vendettas. The match ended with Donegal substitute Tommy Ryan being taken to hospital by ambulance with a suspected broken jaw, some harsh words and threats being offered by one Derry official, who had to be restrained. Kieran McKeever was sent off for the off the ball incident in which Ryan was injured."

In fact Ryan was barely on the pitch, having come on for Manus Boyle, when he was stretched. It made little difference to the result. Despite scoring two goals against the strong wind in the first half, Derry could manage only a single point in the second as Donegal came back to control the midfield exchanges where earlier they had been badly outplayed. Because many of the twelve thousand attendance were arriving late, delayed by border checkpoints, the match was late starting. Two minutes before half time Derry led by 2-2 to 0-4. Dermot McNicholl scored Derry's first goal in the twelfth minute, a good move down the right was worked into the centre, and Damien Barton's shot was followed up by Mick Niblock for a goal. Enda Gormley had the ball in the net two minutes later, but the score was disallowed for a foul on the goalkeeper. Then Dermot Heaney broke powerfully past Matt Gallagher and drove the ball into the net from a narrow angle. Donegal cut the lead back to two points, 2-2 to 0-6, at half time, but it looked as if Derry, with the considerable help of the wind, would continue where they left off in the second half. They got a lot of possession but wasted their chances, and managed only one score in the second half, the best of the match, a long-range point from Enda Gormley.

But this was a significant match. Mickey Moran has no doubt that this was where the decision to win the All-Ireland was made. "After the Donegal fiasco in the quarter-final of the League, when we flopped in the second half, we got together the next Monday night and said we are just going to try everything possible, to look at every avenue to put things right."

Team captain Henry Downey recalls: "Last year we had won the League and we lost out in the most important match of the year, the Ulster championship final. We were going well in the League this year as well and we got to a National League quarter-final. And when we were in the National League quarter-final we certainly tried to win and Donegal tried to beat us. But in hindsight it was of benefit to us.

"Losing to Down in 1991 and Donegal in 1992 was a big disappointment, but it matured the team," Downey says. "We set our sights solely on the first round of the championship game against Down in Newry. It was always going to be an important game, but to get an eleven point victory in difficult circumstances was a big boost to our confidence. Playing Donegal in the Ulster final was a good examination of the team, and we played well enough. Beating both Down and Donegal showed we have the football ability to compete with the best. We had to prove that again and again."

"In 1991 we were not ready," Gary Coleman says. "We were only together for a matter of months. But last year would have been the biggest disappointment, losing the Ulster final. The attitude had to change, the mental approach, the will to eliminate Down and Donegal. It was a case of concentrating on the thought that if they could do it there was no reason why we couldn't."

"Hurtful as it was," Anthony Tohill says, "losing the 1992 Ulster final to Donegal changed attitudes on the Derry team. Although we did win a National League before that, being beaten by Donegal last year was a bitter disappointment for all of the team. It was that defeat against Donegal that was decisive in the make-up of this team. Being a point up and a man ahead at half time and still losing could have broken this team; actually, in view of what Donegal went on to achieve, it just stiffened our resolve. It is just something that I don't think we would ever forget. You always remember getting beaten. It was absolutely devastating. I probably remember more about the 1992 Ulster final, when we lost, than I remember about the 1993 final, when we won. Even worse, I got injured after about twenty minutes and had to come off and to watch the second half of that match and not be able to do anything about it. We let ourselves down, we let the supporters down; it was very disappointing."

Colm O'Rourke once commented about the significance of defeat: "Losing big games can have a significant effect on the mind. Stupid mistakes are remembered and corrected, while the loneliness of being beaten can often toughen the mental resolve to return. After All-Irelands, the pilgrimage home for the vanquished is met at every crossroads and pub with cries of 'We'll be back.' This catch-all phrase is usually already implanted in the mind of the players, who really count."

But Derry were fed up losing to Donegal. "We're not terribly fond of one another," Éamonn Coleman pondered. "Myself and Brian McEniff are totally different types of people. He's a big-time hotelier and I'm an ordinary bricklayer, but we're good friends."

Did the style change? The famous direct football of 1992 gave way to more subtle tactics. Derry have unjustifiably been accused of playing an ancient kick-and-leap game, straight from the days when Mícheál O'Hehir described games on crackly radios with wet and dry batteries: place a skeleton of big players up the middle, root the ball in the air, and hope for the best.

The perception of Derry as a direct team is shaped by the presence of two towering midfielders, Brian McGilligan and Anthony Tohill, as much as by anything else. "I suppose a lot of people thought of Derry teams as big, strong teams," Tohill says. "All they did was hoof the ball seventy yards, and I think it was not a fair reflection on the team. Derry teams can play as good a brand of football as anyone else. I think we have tried to revert away from the old style of hoofing the ball when you get it: we try to concentrate on keeping possession and using the ball, because it is very hard to get it in your hands during a game. You don't see it that often during a match, and you have to make as good a use of it as you can."

"When I came into the scene first, all I had to worry about was catch and kick," Brian McGilligan says. "It was the only type of football player. Now there is so much running, better passing. It was a pity that the 1993 Ulster final was played in such conditions, because on a dry day you would really have seen what this Derry team was capable of. As it was we still showed Donegal that we can play the short game as well as anyone. Before we used to kick the big, hopeful ball into the square and hope for the best. Now we are much more controlled. The emphasis is on a much more open brand of football."

During the 1993 championship county teams began to dream up strategies for coping with the challenge of Tohill and McGilligan at the centre of the field, varying their kick-outs and so on. "It's the sort of thing you expect in club matches," says Tohill. "I used to look forward to inter-county matches and the chance to contest a ball on its own merits."

For Derry men, the 1993 championship reads like a Séamus Heaney poem: two matches for the forwards, two for the backs; Down by 3-11 to 0-9, Monaghan by 0-19 to 0-11, Donegal by 0-8 to 0-6.

Each had their merits; even Monaghan matched Derry for long periods of the Ulster semi-final at Casement Park.

But it was the defeat of Down, with thirteen of their 1991 All-Ireland winning team on board, that thrilled Derry. Dermot Heaney's early goal gave Derry a 1-6 to 0-5 lead at half time, and when Down's John Kelly was sent off twelve minutes from the end, Derry pulled away with goals from Richard Ferris and Éamonn Burns.

Coleman felt he was not going to win the Ulster final by getting involved with Donegal. "I've been preaching discipline for weeks and that's what my players will give me. If someone gets in the way of one of our players running out with the ball, that's a different story; that's too bad."

In fact it was a Donegal man who was sent off in the torrid encounter in Clones, a harsh decision in the eyes of all who braved the rain and the mud to watch. Clones had been upgraded the previous autumn, and parts of it resembled a building site. Even outside the grounds it was a nightmare—a contrast with the free and easy access to Casement Park from the motorway for the previous two years' semi-finals against Monaghan and Down. The rain bucketed down, traffic came to a halt as a large lorry and a long caravan tried to negotiate the streets narrowed by parked cars; the exit roads were log-jammed, bumper to bumper for four hours after the game, and when a minor player was injured there was difficulty getting emergency vehicles out of the ground.

Onfield, the ball was unkickable on the ground, floating on pools of water at times. Fans demanded an explanation why the game was played at all, and why even the minor final was not postponed. Anthony Tohill's performance sank Donegal in the eddy, and Derry hit four points without reply in the opening minutes to effectively finish the matches. Derry missed chances at the end.

"We are sick and tired of hearing that the conditions in that Ulster final suited us," Enda Gormley says. "There is a widespread opinion around that we are a big team and because of that the state of the ground paid a big part in our victory. This is a load of rubbish. We would have been prepared to play on a dry rather than a heavy and wet pitch. We have big players—Anthony Tohill, Brian McGilligan—but there is no question of us all being giants. In the Ulster final it was the smaller players rather than the bigger lads who really did the business. Tohill played well, but so did the smaller players: Kieran McKeever, Karl Diamond, Tony Scullion. That day we adapted better to the conditions. We placed great emphasis on keeping possession."

The All-Ireland semi-final. Now there was a day! You would swear it was Derry that were on home ground. Dublin jittered and panicked, kicking wides and giving away easy scores. At three points up in seven minutes, Derry looked unstoppable. Dublin took twenty-two minutes to get the three points back, outscored them by nine points to one at half time as Jack Sheedy found his stride. Derry put Tony Scullion in on Vinny Murphy. Then, in the half-time dressing-room, Mickey Moran freaked out.

"They weren't doing themselves any justice. All the seventy minutes that they had put in before were gone to waste. They had to get up off their knees. Everything that

had happened in the first half I was able to throw out to
them. I didn't miss anybody. It was getting them up off
their knees that mattered. Their heads were down a bit.
Usually Éamonn roars at them. I usually just come in with
two or three points at the end: how the game should be
played, what we should do tactically out there on the
pitch. Twenty minutes before half time our backs sat back
off them and our midfield stopped working in the middle
of the pitch. We missed three scores, Anthony Tohill,
Damien Barton and Dermot Heaney missed three points,
which would have left us six-nil up. We got in front and
just pushed forward, what Dublin usually do with Keith
Barr and Paul Curran. You can't sit back and let them
away."

Derry came back with a great thirty-five minutes of
football, one to warm the memories of those who
reminisce about Kerry and Dublin in 1977 or Cork and
Dublin in Páirc Uí Chaoimh in 1983. The crowd of 62,643
was more than double what the 1958 team drew to Croke
Park on semi-final day.

That winning point will remain for ever, frozen in slow
motion, in John McGurk's memory. It was natural, the way
the ball came to him, to turn back to his left, but not
natural to kick with his left. Why did he do it? "I was
playing right-half-forward for the kick-outs at the end of
the semi-final, because we wanted Dermot Heaney to play
off Pat Gilroy just for the kick-outs. I wasn't really playing
up front, because once the kick out was taken I would
switch to right-half-back again. The pass from Dermot

McNicholl was too long. It cut out the option of going around Éamonn Heary on the right. The ball ran away from me. I was going towards the Hogan Stand and I remember thinking that I couldn't kick it with my right foot, so I tipped it, and tipped it too high. There was Éamonn Heary standing in front of me, and he stood back a couple of yards and I thought: well, I could turn inside onto my left here."

He had another reason. "During the warm-up I had tried a few shots with my right foot from the same position and missed them. I remembered those misses, and switched it inside to my weaker foot. I turned inside onto my left, and when I hit I thought it just crept inside the post, but when I saw it actually on television it seems to have gone over the centre of the post.

"It was a draw at that stage. If we had been a point down I would have cut inside and gone for a free or something like that ... I knew if we got one score they would have had to get two to win the match, because there didn't seem to be any chance of any team scoring a goal at that stage."

"Did we come down to Dublin just to do what nearly all the past Derry teams have done, or is anyone here willing to go out and die for this one?" Éamonn Coleman enjoined his charges.

"I told youse, I told youse, but youse boys wouldn't listen," Coleman said. "I don't know why youse boys want to talk to me. Sure youse were all tipping Dublin. You've been getting it wrong since Newry. I have been saying for twelve months that we are as good as any team, and we proved that out there. It will be a hell of a final against Cork."

"Genuinely," man of the match Joe Brolly said, "I had insane confidence out there. Even when we were being stuffed I still thought we would win the game. Dublin just seemed to have something vulnerable about them, like they had against Meath in 1991. I can't identify what it is, but there is definitely something there. I mean we are far from a brilliant team, but look at the cut of us for most of the first half. We were swanning around like superstars. We had to cop ourselves on and start playing football. We are not by any means a brilliant team; we can't afford to go out and be admiring ourselves. And I'll tell you what's wrong with Derry: we have no tradition of winning, so when we do win something there is pandemonium.

"You have a sixth sense. You can sense from the crowd. You know when you are winning a game. This is a very stubborn team, you know, very resourceful. In the first half we were doing nothing at all. We had difficulties, you know, particularly in the half-forward line. But once they started to come away it went right. Well, I saw Downey, and Downey is as cute as a fox. I just threw it in to him and I knew he would do something with it."

"What we saw at that moment when we ran on the field," Damien Cassidy said, "should stay with us for the rest of our lives. I would say it was unparalleled in the history of Derry football. Apart from the Hill, it was as if we had the whole ground."

Coleman again: "I asked them to make up their minds and they answered the call. They gave one hell of an effort and that's what they needed to give. When we got two points behind we had it."

And why did Derry dispense with the ceremonial of the semi-final, following the Artane Boys' Band half way along the Cusack Stand and running away before the teams reached Hill 16? In Gaelic football the pre-match parade is a sacred act, of unexplorable origin. Perhaps it is related to the parade of great Celtic athletes or racehorses at the festivals, perhaps to military origins of the IRB. They paraded before the first All-Ireland final in April 1888. They paraded ever since, and when Derry opted out just before the Dubliners took a salute from their fans on Hill 16, it looked like a calculated snub, psychological one-up-manship. "It was an accident," explained Brian McGilligan. "It wasn't planned at all. Someone made a move and we all just automatically ran, thinking the parade was only doing half the pitch. We were all that geared up, that tense about getting it started. It was a bit too late to go back once we had done it." A few on the stands and stepped terraces recalled that the parade was abandoned altogether before the 1958 semi-final because of torrential rain.

Was it a great game? The statisticians reckoned the ball was in play for 25 minutes and 44 seconds of the match, over four minutes less than the much inferior Cork-Mayo semi-final of a week earlier. But the match statistics otherwise compared favourably with recent All-Irelands: 20 per cent fewer stoppages, a longer average sequence of play, fewer aggressive fouls than any final since 1989's Cork and Mayo clash, and the longest average sequence of continuous play since Cork met Meath in 1990. As the intensity of the game increased, the number of unenforced errors went down.

Derry's critics homed in on their scoring. Only two of their forwards scored from play, a total of three points. Six of the Derry points were scored by non-forwards, four by half-backs and by both midfielders. The best forward was Enda Gormley, who kicked a point from play as well as a few good frees. Dublin's five wides at the start of the match were regarded as crucial to Derry's success. "Most of the press stated we scored three points from play," says Enda Gormley. "That's a fact, not an opinion. We still scored fifteen points. The fact that they didn't come from the forwards is possibly worrying. But maybe our midfield and defenders won't score on another occasion. Our forwards started off the year by scoring 3-11 against Down and nineteen points against Monaghan. In the Donegal match, in fairness, the conditions were not great. Donegal are supposed to have a great forward line and they were only capable of scoring six points. At least five of ours were from play; they only got two from play. So it was something to worry about: obviously we need more scores from play and we tried to work on it."

Against Cork, things could hardly be more difficult. Brolly again: "All we can do is think back to Barney Rock's goal to pull back an even better Cork team in 1983, and also their games against Meath. You can take it that Derry will present them with a big physical challenge."

The longest forty-eight hours started with Saturday

morning's departure from Dungiven. A big crowd assembled to send the Oakboys on the way. Some joker paraphrased the Frank McGuinness play: "Observe the sons of Ulster, marching towards the Sam." Another mentioned a prophecy of St Colm Cille. Another carried a message from a unionist friend: "Bring Samuel back to Londonderry." Summit in sight.

Appendix 1

DERRY SENIOR FOOTBALL CHAMPIONSHIP TEAMS 1950–1992

1950 (v. Antrim, first round): C. McGurk; P. Carson, Sonny McCann, J. Kealey, R. McNicholl, Owen Gribben, S. Agnew, Andy Lynch, John Murphy, Charlie Hasson, John Eddie Mullan, Jim Hampson, Pat Keenan, J. Higgins, Peter Kealey.

1951 (v. Cavan): Charlie Moran, Séamus Keenan, Eddie Kealey, T. Doherty, Mickey Gribben, Owen Gribben, John Murphy, Andy Lynch, Larry Higgins, Jim McKeever, Charlie McErlean, Roddy Gribben, J. E. Mullan, Sonny McCann, P. Kiernan.

1952 (v. Monaghan, not complete): Charlie Moran, Jim McKeever, Francie Niblock, Roddy Gribben, John Murphy, Tommy Gribben, Mulholland.

1953 (v. Armagh): J. McGlone, John Murphy, Harry Cassidy, T. Doherty, Mick Gribben, Mick McNaught, Frank Stinson, Jim McKeever, Charlie "Chuck" Higgins, L. Regan, Roddy Gribben, Colm Mulholland, P. Heron, Seán Young, Patsy Breen.

1954 (v. Armagh): John Murphy, T. Doherty, Eddie Kealey, Peter Kealey, Mickey Gribben, Harry Cassidy, Frank Stinson, Jim McKeever, Patsy Breen, Harry Cassidy, T. J. Doherty, T. Gribben, Charlie "Chuck" Higgins, Colm Mulholland, Roddy Gribben. Sub: Emmet Fullen for Mickey Gribben.

1955 (v. Cavan, Ulster final): John Murphy; Hugh Francis Gribben, E. Kealy, T. Doherty; Mickey Gribben 0-1, Harry Cassidy, Frank Stinson; Patsy Breen, Jim McKeever; F. Niblock, T. J. Doherty, Emmet Fullen; Charlie "Chuck" Higgins, Roddy Gribben, Colm Mulholland. Sub: Owen Gribben for Frank Stinson.

1956 (v. Tyrone): Patsy Gormley, E. Muldoon, Eddie Kealey, T. Doherty, Mickey Gribben, Harry Cassidy, Peter Smith, Jim McKeever, Patsy Breen, T. Doherty, Owen Gribben, Phil Stuart, L. Regan, J. E. Mullan, Brendan Murray. Subs: D. O'Kane for Mickey Gribben, T. Stephenson for Cassidy.

1957 (v. Tyrone, Ulster final): Patsy Gormley; Patsy McLarnon, Hugh Francis Gribben, T. Doherty; G. Muldoon, Jim McKeever, Peter Smith; Patsy Breen, Owen Gribben; Seán O'Connell, Roddy Gribben, W. E. Fullen; Harry Cassidy, T. Doherty, Seán Young. Subs: S. O'Connor for Muldoon; Charlie "Chuck" Higgins for Cassidy; Muldoon for Gormley.

1958 (v. Dublin, All-Ireland final): Patsy Gormley; Patsy McLarnon, Hugh Francis Gribben, Tommy Doherty; Patsy Breen, Colm Mulholland, Peter Smith; Jim McKeever (captain), Phil Stuart; Seán O'Connell, Brendan Murray, Denny McKeever; Brian Mullan, Owen Gribben, Charlie "Chuck" Higgins. Subs: Roddy Gribben for Higgins, Leo O'Neill for Mullan, Colm O'Neill for Breen.

1959 (v. Armagh): T. Doherty; Patsy McLarnon, Hugh Francis Gribben, W. Strathearn, Patsy Breen, Colm Mulholland, Peter Smith, Jim McKeever, Leo O'Neill,

T. Scullion, Brendan Murray, Denis McKeever, Brian Mullan, Owen Gribben, W. J. McElhinney. Subs: G. Muldoon for McElhinney, G. O'Neill for Muldoon.

1960 (v. Cavan): P. Gormley; W. O'Kane, Brian Devlin, Brendan Murray; Patsy Breen, Colm Mulholland, Peter Smith; Leo O'Neill, Hugh Francis Gribben; G. O'Neill, Jim McKeever, Denis McKeever, J. O'Neill, T. Scullion, D. J. Cassidy.

1961 (v. Down): Charlie O'Connor; Patsy McLarnon, B. Scullion, Peter Smith; George McGee, Brian Devlin, Hugh Francis Gribben; Willie O'Kane, T. Murray; Seán O'Connell, Jim McKeever, Leo O'Neill; Denis McKeever, Phil Stuart, Brian Rafferty. Sub: Colm Mulholland for Peter Smith.

1962 (v. Tyrone): J. Hasson, Willie O'Kane, Denis Cassidy, C. Donaghy; Colm Mulholland, T. Scullion, Charlie O'Connor, Brian Devlin, Stuart, Seán O'Connell, Jim McKeever, Brian Rafferty, Colm McGuigan, S. O'Neill, J. McNally. Subs: Leo O'Neill for McNally, G. O'Neill for Stuart.

1963 (v. Cavan): Charlie O'Connor, C. Donaghy, Brian Devlin, Brendan Murray, T. Scullion, B. Mullan, S. Devlin, Jim McKeever, Hugh Francis Gribben, Seán O'Connell, Brian Rafferty, Willie O'Kane, Leo O'Neill, Denis McKeever, E. Young. Subs: Colm McGuigan for Young, Dermot Mullan for Donaghy.

1964 (v. Cavan): S. O'Boyle, Éamonn McCann, Hugh Francis Gribben, Charlie O'Connor, Willie O'Kane, T. Scullion, S. Devlin, S. O'Connell, Brian Rafferty, F. Brolly,

Brian Devlin, G. McGuigan, Leo O'Neill, L. Hanfey, Dermot Mullan.

1965 (v. Antrim): Michael Ryan; Des McLarnon, Hugh Francis Gribben, Frank Connolly, Charles O'Connor, Frank Lagan, Frank Kelly, Henry Diamond, Larry Diamond, P. Quinn, Ted McCloskey, Seán O'Connell, Brendan Cassidy, George McGee, M. Duffy. Subs: Colm Murray for Kelly, Austin Mulholland for Connolly, D. Doherty for O'Connor.

1966 (v. Antrim): Séamus Hasson, Des McLarnon, Hugh Francis Gribben, Austin Mulholland, T. Diamond, Malachy McAfee, Phelim McCotter, Séamus Lagan, Henry Diamond, J. J. Kearney, S. McCloskey, B. Casssidy, Seán O'Connell, Charlie O'Connor, Brian Devlin.

1967 (v. Down): Séamus Hasson, Des Mclarnon, Hugh Francis Gribben, Henry Diamond, T. Diamond, Malachy McAfee, P. Gribben, Laurence Diamond, Tom Quinn, B. Cassidy, S. Logan, Mickey Niblock, P. Coleman, S. McCloskey, Seán O'Connell. Subs: J. J. Kearney for Coleman, Mick McGuckian for Cassidy.

1968 (v. Ds, first round): Séamus Hasson; Matt Trolan, Tom Quinn, M. Kelly; T. Diamond, Malachy McAfee, S. Gribben; Tom McGuinness, Séamus Lagan; Mickey Niblock, Brian Devlin, Éamonn Coleman; Colm McGuigan, S. McCloskey, Seán O'Connell. Subs: Gerry O'Loughlin for Gribben, A. McGuckian for McGuigan.

1969 (v. Cavan, semi-final) Séamus Hasson; Matt Trolan, Tom Quinn, M. P. Kelly; Peter Stevenson, Malachy McAfee,

Phelim McCotter; Laurence Diamond, Tom McGuinness; Seán O'Connell, Mickey Niblock, Colm Mullan; Colm McGuigan, Adrian McGuckian, Frank O'Loane.

1970 (Ulster championship winners): Séamus Hasson; Mick McGuckian, Henry Diamond, Tom Quinn; Malachy McAfee, Colm Mullan, Gerry O'Loughlin; Laurence Diamond, Séamus Lagan; Seán O'Connell, Mickey Niblock, Éamonn Coleman; Adrian McGuckian, Brian Devlin, Hughie Niblock. Subs: Anthony McGurk for Mullan, S. Gribben for Hughie Niblock.

1970 (All-Ireland semi-final): Séamus Hasson; Mick McGuckian, Henry Diamond, Matt Trolan; Malachy McAfee, Colm Mullan, Gerry O'Loughlin; Laurence Diamond, Séamus Lagan; Seán O'Connell, Mickey Niblock, Tom Quinn, Adrian McGuckian, Brian Devlin, Hughie Niblock. Subs: Tom McGuinness, Anthony McGurk, Peter Doherty.

1971 (Ulster final v. Down): S. Hassan; Michael McGurk, Henry Diamond, Tom Quinn; Peter Stevenson, Hughie Niblock, Gerry O'Loughlin; Laurence Diamond, S. Gribben; Seán O'Connell, Anthony McGurk, John O'Leary; Adrian McGuckian, Mickey Niblock, E. Coleman. Subs: Malachy McAfee for Hughie Niblock, M. P. Kelly for Quinn, Tom McGuinness for Gribben.

1972 (v. Tyrone): John Somers; Matt Trolan, Tom Quinn, T. Diamond; C. Browne, Mick McGuckian, Gerry O'Loughlin; Tom McGuinness, Laurence Diamond; Anthony McGurk, Colm Mullan, Éamonn Coleman; Adrian McGuckian, Hughie Niblock, Séamus Lagan. Subs: Mickey Moran for Coleman, Malachy McAfee for Mullan.

1973 (v. Down): John Somers; Matt Trolan, Séamus Lagan, Adrian McGuckian; Hugh McGoldrick, Mick McGuckian, Gerry O'Loughlin; Laurence Diamond, Tony Moran; James Convery, Tom McGuinness, Jude Hargan; John O'Leary, Peter Doherty, Seán Donaghy. Subs: Francis Moran for Hugh McGoldrick, Gerry Forrest for Jude Hargan, Anthony McGurk for Seán Donaghy.

1974 (v. Down): John Somers; Mick McGuckian, Séamus Lagan, Adrian McGuckian; F. Stevenson, Hugh McGoldrick, C. Browne; Laurence Diamond, Malachy McAfee; Mickey Moran, Anthony McGurk, Gerry O'Loughlin, Peter Doherty, Tom Quinn, Frank O'Loane.

1975 (Ulster championship winning team): John Somers; Malachy McAfee, Tom Quinn, Gabriel Bradley; Peter Stevenson, Anthony McGurk, Gerry O'Loughlin; Eugene Laverty, Tom McGuinness; Gerry McElhinney, Mickey Lynch, Brendan Kelly; John O'Leary, Seán O'Connell, Mickey Moran. Subs: Séamus Lagan for McAfee, K. Teague for Lagan, Hughie Niblock for McElhinney.

1976 (Ulster championship winning team): John Somers, Liam Murphy, Tom Quinn, Peter Stevenson; Gerry O'Loughlin, Anthony McGurk, Mickey Moran; Tom McGuinness, Laurence Diamond; Brendan Kelly, Mickey Lynch, Fintan McCloskey; John O'Leary, C. Grieve, Gerry McElhinney. Subs: Seán O'Connell for Grieve, Eugene Laverty for Diamond, Gabriel Bradley for O'Loughlin.

1977 (v. Armagh, Ulster final): John Somers; Liam Murphy, Frank Trainor, Gerry Forrest; Gerry O'Loughlin, Anthony McGurk, Gabriel Bradley; Colm McGuigan, Eugene

Laverty; Tom McGuinness, Mickey Lynch, Terence McWilliams; Gerry Keane, Gerry McElhinney, Peter Stevenson. Subs: Cathal Faulkner for Forrest, James McAfee for McGuigan, Fintan McCloskey for McWilliams.

1978 (v. Derry, Ulster semi-final): John Somers, Liam Murphy, Gabriel Bradley, Gerry O'Loughlin, Peter Stevenson, Anthony McGurk, Mickey Moran, Tom McGuinness, Gerry McElhinney, Barney O'Neill, Gerry Keane, Mickey Lynch, Brendan Kelly, Jude Hargan, Denis Kearney. Subs: Eugene Young for McGuinness, Tommy Doherty for Lynch.

1979 (v. Donegal, Ulster semi-final): John Somers, Mickey O'Brien, Gabriel Bradley, P. McElwee, Eugene Donnelly, Anthony McGurk, Denis Kearney, Tommy Doherty, Eugene Young, James McAfee, Jude Hargan, Alfie Dallas, Pat Doherty. Subs: Tom McGuinness for Hargan, Barney O'Neill for Dallas.

1980 (v. Cavan): Mark McFeely; Gabriel Bradley, K. Doherty, P. McElwee; Mickey O'Brien, Anthony McGurk, Barney O'Neill; Tommy Doherty, J. Young; Gerry McElhinney, Hugh McGoldrick, C. McKee; Mickey Lynch, Brendan Kelly, Mickey Moran. Subs: J. McGuinness for McGoldrick.

1981 (v. Down, semi-final): John Somers; Gerry O'Loughlin, Joe Irwin, P. McElwee; Gabriel Bradley, T. Moore, B. O'Neill; Tommy Doherty, Eugene Young; J. McGroarty, Anthony McGurk, James McAfee; Brendan Kelly, M. McFeeley, Mickey Moran. Subs: Mickey Lynch for Moore, Damien Barton for McGroarty, F. Johnson for O'Neill.

1982 (v. Fermanagh): John Somers; Gerry O'Loughlin, J. Treanor, B. Treanor; F. Johnston, Joe Irwin, T. Moore; Tommy Doherty, P. Murphy, B. O'Neill; J. Young, D. Barton, P. Dougan; J. McKee, J. Heaslip. Subs: Pat Doherty for B. Treanor, M. McKee for Colm McKee.

1983 (v. Cavan): John Somers; Peter Doherty, Frank Trainor, P. McElwee; F. Johnston, P. Mackle, A. Scullion; Joe Irwin, Tommy Doherty; Barney O'Neill, K. Quinn, Mickey Lynch; P. Crozier, R. McCusker, K. McWilliams. Subs: Eugene Donnelly for Quinn, K. Quinn for Crozier, P. Murphy for McCusker.

1984 (v. Tyrone): J. Mackle; S. Sands, Joe Irwin, Tony Scullion; Denis Kearney, Frank Trainor, Barney O'Neill; Tommy Doherty, Colm McGuigan; Damien Barton, Gabriel Bradley, Dermot McNicholl; Damien Cassidy, Eugene Young, Declan McNicholl.

1985 (v. Monaghan, Ulster final): J. Mackle; H. McGurk, Tony Scullion, K. Keenan; P. Mackle, B. McPeake, Joe Irwin; P. Murphy, Damien Barton; Dermot McNicholl, E. McElhinney, Declan McNicholl; Damien Cassidy, B. Kealey, T. McGuckian. Subs: Tommy Doherty for McElhinney, E. Rafferty for Cassidy, P. McCormick for Declan McNicholl.

1986 (v. Tyrone): J. Mackle; Joe Irwin, Tony Scullion, H. McGurk; P. Mackle, B. Kealey, P. McCann; P. Murphy, Damien Barton; Dermot McNicholl, E. Gormley, E. McElhinney, C. McKee, Eugene Young, John McGurk.

1987 (Ulster championship winning team): Damien McCusker; H. McGurk, Danny Quinn, Tony Scullion; P. McCormack, Joe Irwin, P. McCann; P. Murphy, Brian McGilligan, Enda Gormley, Dermot McNicholl, Damien Barton, Damien Cassidy, B. Kealey, K. McWilliams. Subs: John McGurk for McWilliams.

1988 (v. Down): Damien McCusker; P. McCormack, D. Quinn, Tony Scullion; John McErlean, Joe Irwin, N. Mullan; P. Murphy, Brian McGilligan; P. Young, Enda Gormley, P. Kealey; Damien Cassidy, Eugene Young, Séamus Downey. Subs: Kieran McKeever for McErlean (16 mins.), Damien Barton for Eugene Young (24 mins.), Dermot McNicholl for P. Young.

1989 (v. Donegal, semi-final): C. McKenna; B. Young, Danny Quinn, Tony Scullion; B. McPeake, Joe Irwin, Kieran McKeever; P. Murphy, Brian McGilligan; Damien McCusker, B. Kealey, Damien Cassidy; Enda Gormley, Damien Barton, A. Quigg. Subs: Séamus Downey for McCusker (43 mins.), P. J. McCormack for Quinn (45 mins.), R. Ferris for Quigg (57 mins.).

1990 (v. Donegal): Damien McCusker; E. Kelly, Danny Quinn, Tony Scullion, John McGurk; Kieran McKeever, N. Mullan, P. Murphy, Brian McGilligan, P. Barton, Damien Barton, Damien Cassidy, Enda Gormley, Séamus Downey, Fergal McCusker. Subs: Gerry McElhinney for Murphy, T. McGuckian for Mullan, Joe Brolly for P. Barton.

1991 (v. Down): Damien McCusker; Fergal McCusker, Tony Scullion, John McGurk; Kieran McKeever, Danny Quinn, Henry Downey; Anthony Tohill, Brian McGilligan, Dermot

McNicholl; Dermot Heaney, Enda Gormley; Éamonn Burns, Damien Barton, Colm McGurk. Subs: Joe Brolly for Heaney, Gary Coleman for Colm McGurk, Séamus Downey for Éamonn Burns.

1992 (v. Donegal, Ulster final): Damien McCusker; Kieran McKeever, Danny Quinn, Tony Scullion; John McGurk, Henry Downey, Gary Coleman; Brian McGilligan, Dermot Heaney; Anthony Tohill 0-1, Dermot McNicholl 0-1, Damien Cassidy; Declan Bateson, Séamus Downey 1-0, Enda Gormley. Subs: Damien Barton 0-1 for Tohill, John McErlean for Quinn, Joe Brolly for Bateson.

SENIOR HURLING

1990 (v. Down): P. Ó Mianáin, C. McGurk, C. Murray, K. McKeever, C. McGurk, Brian McGilligan, N. Mullan, D. Mulholland, Tony Scullion, D. Cassidy, M. Cassidy, M. Cartin, J. McGurk, S. Sands, Henry Downey. Subs: J. Brawley for Scullion, R. O'Kane for C. McGurk, H. Downey for Cartin.

1991 (v. Down): P. Ó Mianáin, K. McGurk, Seán Sands, Emmet Downey, G. McGilligan, Mark Cassidy, A. McCrystal, H. McCosker, M. Cartin, Oliver Collins, Declan Cassidy, F. Burke, R. McCloskey, Brendan Regan, P. Cassidy. Sub: L. McGowan for A. McCrystal.

Appendix 2

DERRY SENIOR FOOTBALL CHAMPIONS

1905	Clann Uladh (*attr.*)	1938	Lavey
1906	Clan Uladh (*attr.*)	1939	Magherafelt Dungiven
1907	Éire Óg	1940	Newbridge
1908	Éire Óg	1941	Ballinascreen
1913/14	Clan Chonaill (*attr.*)	1942	Magherafelt
1916	Sarsfields	1943	Lavey
1917	St Patrick's	1944	Lavey
1918	Emmets	1945	Newbridge
1921	Derry Guilds	1946	Magherafelt
1922	Emmets (*attr.*)	1947	Dungiven
1925	Magherafelt (*attr.*)	1949	Magherafelt
1926/27	Ballinderry	1950	Newbridge
1928	Glenullin	1951	Dungiven
1930	Buncrana	1952	Éire Óg
1931	Burt	1953	Desertmartin
1933	*No championship*	1954	Lavey
1934	Ballinascreen	1955	Newbridge
1935	Ballinascreen	1956	Bellaghy
1936	Loup	1957	Ballerin
1937	Newbridge (*on objection*)	1958	Bellaghy
		1959	Bellaghy
		1960	Bellaghy
		1961	Bellaghy (*on objection*)

1962	Ballymaguigan	1978	Magherafelt
1963	Bellaghy	1979	Bellaghy
1964	Bellaghy	1980	Ballinderry
1965	Bellaghy	1981	Ballinderry
1966	Newbridge	1982	*Void*
1967	Newbridge	1983	Dungiven
1968	Bellaghy	1984	Dungiven
1969	Bellaghy	1985	Glenullin
1970	Newbridge	1986	Bellaghy
1971	Bellaghy	1987	Dungiven
1972	Bellaghy	1988	Lavey
1973	Ballinascreen	1989	Newbridge
1974	Ballinderry	1990	Lavey
1975	Bellaghy	1991	Dungiven
1976	Ballerin	1992	Lavey
1977	Lavey		

Appendix 3

DERRY'S CHAMPIONSHIP RECORD

1903: Tyrone w.o. from Derry

1904: Derry w.o. from Donegal

1905: 10 Feb. 1906 Derry 1-3 Tyrone 0-2 (may refer to
1904 SFC; no further records)

1906: Derry w.o. from Donegal, 18 Aug. Antrim 1-14
Derry 0-4 Belfast

1910: 8 May Tyrone w.o. from Derry

1914: Monaghan 3-2 Derry 0-3 Derry

1916: 2 July Monaghan beat Derry, Clones

1917: 20 May Cavan beat Derry, Derry

1918: 28 Apr. Antrim 4-1 Derry 2-4 Belfast

1919: 25 May Derry 2-4 Fermanagh 0-3 Wattlebridge;
1 June Antrim 1-4 Derry 1-1 Derry

1920: 23 May Derry 0-11 Donegal 0-7 Derry; 23 July
Cavan beat Derry, Belturbet

1921: 13 Nov. Derry 2-1 Donegal 0-3 Strabane; 11 Dec.
Derry 1-4 Antrim 0-3 Derry; 28 Oct. 1923 Monaghan
2-2 Derry 0-1 Clones

1922: 13 Aug. Cavan 4-4 Derry 1-1 Cavan

1923: 17 June Derry 1-3 Donegal 1-2 Letterkenny; Derry
disqualified

1926: 6 June Tyrone 3-3 Derry 2-1 Dungannon

1927: 22 May Cavan 7-7 Derry 4-3 Belfast

1928: 27 May Tyrone 7-3 Derry 2-3 Dungannon

1945: 10 June Donegal 3-7 Derry 2-3 Letterkenny

1946: 9 June Derry 4-6 Fermanagh 0-4 Magherafelt;
       30 June Antrim 1-11 Derry 0-10 Corrigan Park

1947: 15 June Down 2-11 Derry 2-5 Lurgan

1948: 6 June Monaghan 2-9 Derry 2-6 Clones

1949: 4 June Antrim 5-9 Derry 1-6 Magherafelt

1950: 4 June Antrim 5-10 Derry 0-5 Corrigan Park

1951: 24 June Derry 1-3 Monaghan 0-5 Magherafelt; 8 July
       Cavan 1-6 Derry 1-4 Lurgan 7,000

1952: 22 June Monaghan 2-12 Derry 0-12 Clones

1953: 30 May Derry 1-11 Down 2-5 Magherafelt; 12 July
       Armagh 4-11 Derry 1-5 Casement Park

1954: 13 June Derry 4-11 Down 3-4 Newcastle; 4 July
       Armagh 1-12 Derry 1-6 Casement Park

1955: 5 June Derry 0-13 Tyrone 1-5 Magherafelt 4,500;
       3 July Derry 3-4 Armagh 0-2 Casement Park; 31 July
       Cavan 1-11 Derry 0-8 Clones 24,800

1956: 3 June Tyrone 3-7 Derry 2-4 Dungannon

1957: 9 June Derry 4-14 Antrim 0-8 Ballinascreen; 7 July
       Derry 1-10 Cavan 1-9 Dungannon; 28 July Tyrone
       1-9 Derry 0-10 Clones 36,500

1958: 1 June Derry 0-8 Antrim 0-5 Casement Park; 13 July
       Derry 4-7 Cavan 3-6 Clones 6,000; 27 July Derry
       1-11 Down 2-4 Clones 22,000; 24 Aug. Derry 2-6
       Kerry 2-5 Croke Park 30,723; 28 Sept. Dublin 1-12
       Derry 1-9 Croke Park 73,371

1959: 31 May Armagh 1-6 Derry 0-5 Lurgan 5,000

1960: 5 June Derry 3-10 Armagh 1-9 Magherafelt 6,000;
       17 July Cavan 3-6 Derry 0-5 Casement Park 8,000

1961: 28 May Derry 2-10 Donegal 0-4 Ballybofey; 11 June
       Derry 1-9 Tyrone 0-10 Ballinascreen 4,000; 2 July
       Down 2-12 Derry 1-10 Belfast 18,000

1962: 3 June Derry 2-10 Donegal 2-7 Magherafelt 3,000;
21 June Tyrone 1-9 Derry 2-2 Dungannon

1963: 23 June Cavan 3-9 Derry 2-8 Ballinascreen 6,000

1964: 14 June Cavan 3-9 Derry 2-3 Cavan 2,000

1965: 30 May Antrim 2-9 Derry 2-6 Ballinascreen

1966: 5 June Antrim 2-7 Derry 0-6 Belfast

1967: 11 June Down 3-9 Derry 1-10 Newry

1968: 9 June Down 1-8 Derry 1-6 Ballinascreen

1969: 1 June Derry 2-8 Tyrone 0-8 Dungannon; 29 June
Cavan 2-3 Derry 0-9 Clones

1970: 7 June Derry 3-12 Tyrone 0-7 Ballinascreen; 28 June
Derry 1-8 Cavan 1-5 Irvinestown; 26 July Derry 2-13
Antrim 1-12 Clones; 23 Aug. Kerry 0-23 Derry 0-10
Croke Park 38,045

1971: 6 June Derry 4-10 Fermanagh 1-10 Ballinascreen;
20 June Down 3-14 Derry 3-6 Newry

1972: 4 June Derry 5-7 Fermanagh 0-7 Irvinestown;
25 June Derry 2-9 Antrim 2-5 Ballinascreen; 9 July
Tyrone 1-8 Derry 0-9 Dungannon

1973: 3 June Derry 1-7 Monaghan 0-5 Castleblayney;
15 July Down 1-12 Derry 0-9 Lurgan

1974: 9 June Derry 3-6 Monaghan 0-8 Ballinascreen;
14 July Down 1-12 Derry 0-7 Lurgan

1975: 22 June Derry 2-15 Armagh 1-7 Omagh; 6 July Derry
1-11 Monaghan 1-11 Dungannon; 13 July Derry
0-14 Monaghan 1-6 Dungannon (R); 27 July Derry
1-16 Down 2-6 Clones 25,000; 24 Aug. Dublin 3-13
Derry 3-8 Croke Park 44,455

1976: 13 June Derry 1-19 Armagh 2-1 Omagh; 27 June
Derry 0-12 Tyrone 0-8 Clones; 18 July Derry 1-8
Cavan 1-8 Clones 20,000; 25 July Derry 0-22 Cavan
1-16 Clones 25,000 (Replay, extra time); 9 Aug.
Kerry 5-14 Derry 1-10 Croke Park 30.963

1977: 29 May Derry 1-12 Donegal 0-12 Ballybofey; 19 June
Derry 3-10 Tyrone 1-11 Lurgan; 3 July Derry 0-10
Down 0-8 Clones; 24 July Armagh 3-10 Derry 1-5
Clones 25,000

1978: 28 May Derry 3-12 Donegal 0-7 Ballinascreen;
18 June Derry 3-11 Tyrone 0-9 Lurgan; 2 July Down
1-14 Derry 2-8 Casement Park

1979: 10 June Derry 2-12 Cavan 1-13 Cavan; 1 July
Donegal 2-9 Derry 0-14 Omagh

1980: 8 June Cavan 2-9 Derry 2-7 Ballinascreen

1981: 7 June Derry 0-12 Fermanagh 0-10 Ballinascreen;
5 July Down 0-12 Derry 0-9 Clones

1982: 6 June Fermanagh 1-9 Derry 1-8 Irvinestown

1983: 22 May Cavan 1-12 Derry 0-11 Ballinascreen

1984: 27 May Derry 1-13 Cavan 0-14 Cavan; 10 June
Tyrone 1-13 Derry 3-4 Ballinascreen

1985: 2 June Derry 1-9 Tyrone 1-8 Ballinascreen; 23 June
Derry 0-11 Cavan 0-7 Armagh; July Monaghan 2-9
Derry 0-8 Clones

1986: 2 June Tyrone 2-6 Derry 1-7 Omagh

1987: 31 May Derry 1-12 Down 2-7 Newry; 21 June Derry
2-7 Cavan 1-10 Omagh 14,000; 5 July Derry 2-11
Cavan 2-8 Omagh (R); 19 July Derry 0-11 Armagh
0-9 Clones; 23 Aug. Meath 0-15 Derry 0-8 Croke
Park 40,285

1988: 29 May Down 1-11 Derry 0-7 Ballinascreen 8,000

1989: 28 May Derry 4-15 Fermanagh 1-7 Irvinestown
4,000; 18 June Donegal 2-8 Derry 1-9 Clones

1990: 27 May Derry 4-14 Fermanagh 1-7 10,000; 17 June
Donegal 1-15 Derry 0-8 5,000

1991: 26 May Derry 1-9 Tyrone 1-8 Derry 12,000; 16 June
Derry 0-13 Monaghan 0-8 Derry 10,000; 30 June
Down 0-13 Derry 1-10 Armagh 10,000; 14 July
Down 0-14 Derry 0-9 Armagh 10,000

1992: 17 May Derry 1-10 Tyrone 1-7 Derry 12,000; 14 June
Derry 1-14 Monaghan 3-8 Castleblayney 8,000;
21 June Derry 2-9 Monaghan 0-7 Derry 10,000;
28 June Derry 0-15 Down 0-12 Casement Park
30,000; 19 July Donegal 0-14 Derry 1-9 Clones
30,000

1993: 30 May Derry 3-11 Down 0-9 Newry 17,000; 20 June
Derry 0-19 Monaghan 0-11 Casement Park 20,000;
18 July Derry 0-8 Donegal 0-6 Clones 27,000;
22 Aug. Derry 0-15 Dublin 0-14 Croke Park 62,643.

Appendix 4

THE 1993 CHAMPIONSHIP CAMPAIGN

30 May: Derry 3-11 Down 0-9 Newry. Ulster first round. Damien McCusker, John McGurk, Danny Quinn, Tony Scullion, Karl Diamond, Henry Downey, Gary Coleman, Anthony Tohill 0-4, Brian McGilligan, Richard Ferris 1-0, Damien Barton 0-1, Damien Cassidy 0-3, Dermot McNicholl, Dermot Heaney 1-0, Enda Gormley 0-2. Subs: Fergal McCusker for Scullion, Éamonn Burns 1-1 for McNicholl.

20 June: Derry 0-19 Monaghan 0-11 Casement Park. Ulster semi-final. Damien McCusker, Tony Scullion, Danny Quinn, Kieran McKeever, Karl Diamond 0-1, Henry Downey, Gary Coleman, Brian McGilligan 0-1, Anthony Tohill 0-5, Richard Ferris, Damien Barton, Damien Cassidy 0-1, Éamonn Burns, Dermot Heaney 0-1, Enda Gormley 0-7, Subs: Brian McCormack for Ferris, Joe Brolly 0-3 for Burns, Fergal McCusker for Quinn.

18 July: Derry 0-8 Donegal 0-6 Clones. Ulster final. Damien McCusker, Kieran McKeever, Tony Scullion, Gary Coleman, Fergal McCusker, Henry Downey, John McGurk, Anthony Tohill 0-1, Brian McGilligan, Brian McCormack, Damien Barton 0-1, S. Mulvenna, Damien Cassidy 0-2, Dermot Heaney, Enda Gormley 0-3. Subs: Dermot McNicholl 0-1 for Heaney, Joe Brolly for Mulvenna, Karl Diamond for McNicholl.

22 August: Derry 0-15 Dublin 0-14 Croke Park. All-Ireland semi-final. Damien McCusker, Kieran McKeever, Danny Quinn, Tony Scullion, John McGurk 0-1, Henry Downey 0-2, Gary Coleman 0-1, Anthony Tohill 0-2, Brian McGilligan 0-1, Dermot Heaney, Damien Barton, Damien Cassidy, Joe Brolly 0-1, Séamus Downey, Enda Gormley 0-7. Subs: Karl Diamond for Quinn, Dermot McNicholl for Cassidy, Fergal McCusker for Barton.

19 September: Derry 1-14 Cork 2-8 Croke Park. All-Ireland final. Damien McCusker, Kieran McKeever, Tony Scullion, Gary Coleman, John McGurk 0-2, Henry Downey, Fergal McCusker, Anthony Tohill 0-3, Brian McGilligan 0-1, Dermot Heaney, Damien Barton, Damien Cassidy, Joe Brolly 0-1, Séamus Downey 1-0, Enda Gormley 0-6. Subs: Dermot McNicholl 0-1 for Cassidy, Éamonn Burns for Séamus Downey.